Experiencing Good Friday

Meditations on the Seven Last Words of Jesus

GAYLENE BAIER

Copyright © 2018 Gaylene Baier
All rights reserved.

Published in the United States of America

ISBN-13: 978-1727766172
ISBN-10: 1727766172

DEDICATION

For Bill Baier

My precious husband of sixty years who has taught me about God's unconditional love.

ACKNOWLEDGEMENTS

A special "Thank you" to Nancy Parsons for her patience, encouragement and technical skills. Thank you to Gerri Kirkpatrick for her editing. Thank you to my family for their support and attendance every Good Friday as a "New Word" was presented. These Words could never have been proclaimed without the speaking of Jesus' words by Dennis O'Connor and Ric Cross. And, most importantly, thank you Jesus for the powerful words you proclaimed.

TABLE OF CONTENTS

FORWARD 7

Standing at the Foot of the Cross, A Process For Healing 9
Simon of Cyrene 15
Veronica 21
The Crucifier 27
Roman Soldier 33
Peter 39
Anonymous By-Stander 45
Mary of Magdala 51
Dismas 57
Mother of Zebedee's Sons 63
The Beloved Disciple 69
John, Son of Thunder 77
Nicodemus 83
Joseph of Arimathea 89
People of Sacred Heart Parish 95
Mary, Our Mother 101
Mary, Wife of Clopas 107
The Centurion 113
Jesus Christ 119
God the Father 125
POEM: Father Is It Time? 131

FORWARD

My Journey with the Passion of Jesus Christ

As a child, I heard the Redemptorist Priests as they gave retreats at our church speaking on the Seven Last Words of Jesus. When I was a young girl, I had the habit of walking to church on the Saturdays of Lent to pray the Stations of the Cross and then go to confession. In high school, I read a book called *A Doctor at Calvary* by Pierre Barbet, M.D. These three experiences laid a foundation of respect, awe and love for Jesus and His last hours on earth. His Seven Last Words found a place in my heart. Their meanings have grown richer over the years.

The Stations of the Cross taught me about journeying. We are a pilgrim people on the journey home. That journey always includes pain and suffering, something that all of us would prefer to avoid. Jesus didn't avoid His path. He wrestled with His Father in the Garden, but accepted the Father's Will even as it led to the cross. Pierre Barbet, a surgeon, did careful studies of the Shroud of Turin, believed to be Jesus' burial cloth, before publishing His book.

Pierre speaks of Jesus' death from an anatomical viewpoint. He reports what the person is experiencing within His body as He dies from crucifixion. After my first reading of this book, I could never look at the cross in the same manner. It became my book of meditation for many Lents. It was my privilege to go to Turin, Italy and view the Shroud, a most humbling experience. His physical suffering is recorded there.

The Words of Jesus fascinate me. What love, what grit, what compassion spoke those Words? Jesus is the Word made flesh. His dying Words are important to me. They teach, encourage, support, sustain and love me into greater and greater graces. I trust this book will enrich your love for His Words.

This book is a collection of meditations about various persons standing near or at the cross of Jesus. Choosing a different person, I would pray daily trying to imagine how they felt hearing Jesus speak His Words. After a year of prayer with them, I would write their meditation. May you be blessed by their words.

Standing at the Foot of the Cross

A Process for Healing with the

Seven Last Words of Jesus

When I was taking my certification for Spiritual Direction, one of my assignments was to look over my life and chose a symbol that represented it. I choose the cross. It seems that my life has been a series of either being on the cross, standing at the foot of the cross with another, or looking to Jesus on the cross and seeking His forgiveness for my many sins. His words always seemed to be carefully chosen when He spoke. I figure that whatever He spoke on the cross had to be really important or He would never have spoken them. I believe His Seven Words are the framework for our seven steps to victory. This is the path our Savior traveled. This is the path I believe we are called to travel.

A grace I have been given is the grace to remember and reflect on the last Seven Words of Jesus on a daily basis. I can't begin to tell you the many graces, insights, and absolute joy these words have brought me. Each year, I pray these words from the viewpoint of someone who stood at the foot of the cross, as Jesus was crucified. Then I write a meditation from my reflections. On Good Friday, I am privileged to share my meditation of the Seven Words with our congregation at our Good Friday Way of the Cross.

I want to speak to you about those words on the cross and how I see them as a way to deeper, more complete healing in ourselves and hopefully to those we minister to. Sometimes, I see myself stuck at a certain word. As I ponder that word, I begin to see my resistance.

I would like you to think for a moment about those words. Do you know all Seven? As a reminder they are, "Father forgive them, they know not what they do." "This day you will be in paradise." "Woman, behold your son. Son, behold your Mother." "My God, my God, why have you forsaken me?" "I thirst." "It is finished." "Father, into your hands I commend my spirit." Which one stands out to you today? Which one do you have the most trouble with today? Which one comforts today? Which one is the most difficult for you to speak today?

I can see the Seven Words combating the seven Capitol sins. Those sins are anger, envy, lust, pride, gluttony, sloth and avarice.

"FATHER FORGIVE THEM. THEY KNOW NOT WHAT THEY DO."

Can you really call your God Father? Do you have an intimate relationship with Him or is it more distant? In our older generations, fathers were bread winner. They were short on conversation and expressing feelings. These made intimate relationships nearly impossible. Forgiveness, that's a word that usually is difficult for us to swallow. We are "good" Christian people, we say we want to forgive and we wait for ourselves to "feel" forgiving. That usually doesn't happen. Forgiveness is an act of the will. We choose it. Feeling usually follows, but NOT always immediately. Can we allow ourselves to see from the other's point of view and realize that they don't have a clue how they are hurting us? Can we begin to see why healing is so difficult? Just this first word has enough challenge in it to keep us pondering for a long time.

ANGER- Unforgiveness is anger out of control. Seven times seventy times we are called to forgive.

Father, we want to imitate Jesus. You know those we have chosen not to forgive, ourselves included. Please, we are tired of our anger. It is so destructive. This day, give us the grace to choose to forgive. Father, forgive them. They don't understand, but we do.

"THIS DAY YOU'LL BE IN PARADISE WITH ME."

If we have truly embraced that first word, then it follows that "the enemy", the one to whom we have offered forgiveness deserves to be in paradise with us. Paradise is that place where Adam and Eve lived before they succumbed to their temptations and sinned. This word is the litmus test of the first word. Can we offer our enemy that degree of forgiveness? Can we allow the healing plan of God to take place deep within us? Can we choose to love as Jesus did? I need to pray for my "enemy" that they may enjoy Paradise this day.

ENVY- I want first place. I deserve it, they don't.

Jesus, we need to pray for our "enemy" that they enjoy Paradise today. Please help us to desire that no one is excluded from Paradise. In our selfishness, our envy, we always want to be first and have the best, but you want everyone to enjoy Paradise. Jesus, may we always desire that all of our brothers and sisters come into your Paradise.

"WOMAN, BEHOLD YOUR SON. SON, BEHOLD YOUR MOTHER."

Who is this woman? Remember that once folks asked Jesus, who is your Mother. His reply was whoever did the will of the Father was mother to Him. The woman at the cross is the new Eve. She is the one, who in all humility, could say, "Let it be done according to God's will." "Do whatever He tells you." She is obedient. Who is this Son? He/she is the Beloved Disciple. Disciples follow their master, learning as they go. Jesus tells that disciple, behold her. To behold is to observe, to look at, and to see. Look at her purity. Imitate her. He tells the woman, behold your son. Observe him. He is behaving as you did. He is pure of heart. Help him to stay that way. Remember, it is in our will that we chose to live in purity of heart, body and soul. We are called to purity on all levels of our being. Purity renounces all unlawful pleasures. Purity of heart renounces lust, that desire to want what we want.

LUST—is unlawful pleasures, especially of the senses.

Jesus, we call your Mother the Immaculate Conception. From her conception she was a pure vessel. Jesus, we want to be your Beloved. Grant us the grace to continually chose purity of body, soul and spirit. We chose to renounce all unlawful pleasures.

"MY GOD, MY GOD, WHY HAVE YOU FORSAKEN ME?"

Remember the woman. She said yes, but I wonder if she knew her "Yes" would lead to seeing her son on a cross. When we say "yes" to a situation, we will have to face the darkness of forsakenness. In saying "yes" to Jesus, we have said "no" to our way. We begin to see the depth of our will and our selfishness. We begin to see our own sinfulness. Sin separates us from God. That separation makes us feel forsaken. We have lost control over that which we had no control of in the first place. Most of us fight the feelings of forsakenness. It is our pride that calls for independence from God.

PRIDE—It is independence from God. In our forsaken state we met our limitations. We are humbled.

Father, in our forsaken state we meet our limitations. We are humbled. Everything inside us abhors forsakenness. Let us remember what we pray, "your kingdom come, your will be done." Give us courage when we experience our sinfulness which separates us from you

"I THIRST."

It is only in the darkness of a situation, where I feel forsaken, that I discover my deepest thirst. What is most needed in this situation? What do I need to cry out for? It seems to me that when I allow myself to really experience the pain of a situation, I can begin to see more clearly what is most needed. That's what I need to thirst for the most. But sometimes, when we cry out in our thirst we are offered something unpleasant to drink. What is the bitterness I am being offered to drink in this situation? Am I willing to accept it?

GLUTTONY—We thirst for what satisfies ourselves, instead of what satisfies God and His command to love.

Father, Jesus was thirsting to drink the "New Wine" of your Kingdom. In our selfishness, we chose our addictions and false gods. We chose to glutton on that which never satisfies. Father, grant us the grace to want you kingdom to come in us. We want to thirst for what satisfies your will.

"IT IS FINISHED"

When I know the resistance, the pain, the brokenness or the sin I am dealing with, then, I know it is finished. Jesus once said not to worry so much about the splinter in your brother's eye, but rather to pay attention to the plank in your own. When I can see clearly the plank in my eye and name it, then it is finished. Naming something gives us power over it. I know what has stood in the way of my relationship with God and my brothers and sisters. It is perseverance to the very end. It is finished. The battle is over.

SLOTH has many faces. Laziness, I'll do it tomorrow attitude. Lack of commitment.

Father, we are people of procrastination. Tomorrow is better, even though your word says, "Today is the Day of Salvation." Grant us the grace to persevere in our desire for holiness. Help us to name what we need in our lives. Help us to defeat the sloth of our lives.

"FATHER, INTO YOUR HANDS, I COMMEND MY SPIRIT."

Now we can truly release the entire situation into the Father's hands. We can name it, so we can put it into His loving hands. It has been a struggle. It has been painful. It took much energy. But we know with what we have battled, and we know the battle is finished. We can safely choose to put our spirit into the Father's hands. We are so fearful of detaching, but our Father can be trusted

AVARICE--Giving over our greatest attachment, our addictions, and our idols. We are so fearful of detachment.

Father help us to detach from everything. We desire only you and your Kingdom. Father, Jesus had to detach from everything, except your will. There was no avarice in Him. In complete confidence He could give all over to you.

If I can choose to stick with the process of dying as Jesus did, I can be assured of the victory. I can embrace death on a cross for the Father's glory. Jesus shows me the way to the Father. His Seven Last Words are the pattern for dying to the Seven Capitol sins in my life. May I willingly embrace my crosses with these same Words.

The Last Seven Words

as heard by

Simon of Cyrene

Jesus spoke seven times from the cross, or His Seven Last Words. These words have been handed down over the centuries for our remembrance. Today, I invite you to stop awhile and reflect on these words. Allow the Holy Spirit to take you deeper into the meaning of these words of Jesus. Every word spoken by Jesus is life for the listener.

I have a story to tell you on this day that you remember the death of Jesus. It is a most unusual story. I was there. I watched it all. I'll never forget that day. It changed my life forever. My name is Simon. I come from Cyrene. Cyrene is a long distance from Jerusalem. I had traveled many days on our journey to Jerusalem. My wife and our two sons, Alexander and Rufus were with me. Traveling was difficult and tiring, but we wanted to come to Jerusalem for the Passover. Every good Jew dreams of the day they can come to Jerusalem to remember what our Father Moses did on that night so long ago. I anticipated this journey. No difficulty could take the joy that was in my heart.

The city was crowded with fellow travelers. It was so exciting. We were just coming in from the fields, and as we approached the city, we could see a crowd of people with the Roman soldiers. There was much shouting and commotion. Then we saw what was happening. The Romans were taking this man to be crucified. He was carrying a cross. Before I had a chance to take it all in, a Roman soldier yelled at me. "Help Him!", he shouted. Dumbfounded, I came forward. One does not argue with the LAW. They put a crossbeam on my shoulder and I followed along behind this man.

My head was spinning. How could Yaweh allowed this to happen to me? I am a good Jew. I keep the law. Why would I be humiliated like this? Who is this man? There is a large crowd of people following after us. Who are they? Why are they following Him? They are lamenting and beating their breasts over Him. What man deserves such a show of sorrow? Look at His clothes. They are blood stained. Surely, He must have been scourged. What terrible crime has He committed?

I was tired and confused by the things I observed as we stumbled together to the hill. I was filled with fear. Crucifixion is a cruel business. When we got to the hill, the soldiers took the crossbeam from me. Thank goodness, they dismissed me with no further words. My wife and sons had followed behind me as we walked to this hill. What a relief to be in their company again! They wanted to hurry away, but I could not leave. This man is like no man I've ever met before. I was compelled to stay. I'd heard the crowd say His name. They called him Jesus. I'd heard about Him in Cyrene. Once a man came through our town saying he'd been healed by Jesus over by Galilee. The latest prophet and miracle worker always captures the attention of us.

"FATHER, FORGIVE THEM. THEY KNOW NOT WHAT THEY DO."

"What kind of man is this? Does He not know the law of our Fathers, an eye for an eye, a tooth for a tooth? What is this foolishness of forgiveness? Those Romans are always persecuting us Jews. They are the enemy. Why would you ever forgive an enemy? What kind of a man is He? But His voice and His words carry such authority. He truly asks that they be forgiven. What is that you say? Someone nearby me is saying that He taught that you should forgive seven times seventy times. What foolishness is this? They don't know what they are doing. Ha! I've never seen a Roman who didn't know what cruelty they were doing. Our enemies always know what they are doing to us. Forgive them. Never!

Dear Jesus, can you see my hard heart? I, too, have enemies. They hurt me in so many ways. I've told you and anyone else who will listen to me, about the injustice I suffer. And what about those people who get away with their sins? Yes, I know, sometimes I'm my own worst enemy. It is not easy to forgive myself. You speak hard words to me when you speak of forgiveness.

"THIS DAY YOU WILL BE WITH ME IN PARADISE."

What blasphemy is He speaking now? Everyone knows that when Adam sinned, God banished him from paradise. Paradise is that beautiful Garden of Yaweh. Everything was beautiful then, but it is not that way any more. Life is difficult. It surely isn't any paradise. When He spoke before He directed His prayer to His Father. Now He is offering that man next to him paradise. Who does He think He is? He acts like He has a right to offer paradise. Yaweh is the only one who can open the way and He closed it after Adam sinned. How dare He call God His Father? This man speaks strange words. Yet there is something about Him that intrigues me.

Dear Jesus, you know who you are. You know who the Father is. You are in an intimate relationship with Him. Freely you chose to become man. Freely you chose to lay down your life. That thief upon the cross confessed His sinfulness. There is no stealing into your paradise. Only in confessing my sin and accepting your work on the cross can I hear your words of promise. You promise Paradise to your followers.

"WOMAN, BEHOLD YOUR SON. SON, BEHOLD YOUR MOTHER."

That's who that woman is, His mother. When we were walking here, He fell once. I never thought He'd have the strength to get up again. But He raised His head and there stood this woman. They looked at each other like two lovers. Not a word was spoken, but you could feel strength return to Him. There was this man next to her when all this happened. That's who He is talking to now. I guess He knows He is about to die and wants to get His affairs taken care of before that happens.

Dear Jesus, how deaf we are to some of your words. We hear without hearing. On the cross you commissioned your mother to be mother of us believers. She is symbol of the Church, Holy Mother Church. She cares for us like any good mother. She loves us tenderly and desires to see us grow in our faith. We are sons and daughters of Holy Mother Church. Increase our ability to hear and believe what you speak to us through the guidance of the church.

"MY GOD, MY GOD, WHY HAVE YOU FORSAKEN ME?"

"I understand! I understand! How blind I've been! How deaf I've been! On the cross above His head is a sign that reads, "King of the Jews". I scoffed at that sign before, but now I believe. This is the Messiah! Did you not hear? He was calling to God in the words of our Psalms. I see what I couldn't see before. He lives the words of the Psalm. His hands and feet are pierced. All His bones can be counted. The Romans cast lots for His clothes. It is all there. It is the Messiah! He is my Messiah, my King!

Father God, take the deafness from our ears. Open our eyes that we might see and believe that your only Begotten Son is our Lord, Our God, Our Savior and Our King. Jesus knew who He was. He knew He was the Suffering Servant. He knew upon the cross the reality of the words prophesied so long ago. Help us to know who He is in our lives. Jesus is deserving of all our love. Jesus is deserving of all of our adoration. Jesus is deserving of all of our worship. Jesus is the one we are called to serve. King Jesus, help us to be your faithful servants.

"I THIRST."

Our Psalm says, "My throat is dried up like baked clay, my tongue cleaves to my jaws; to the dust of death you have brought me down." Crucifixion does that to a person. I have heard men scream in their agony of thirst. Remember I crossed the Sinai to get to Jerusalem. My people know about thirst. The desert teaches one to appreciate and cherish "Living Water". This Psalm also says of the Messiah that He is like water poured out. He was offered drugged wine, but He refuses it. Jesus thirsts for something more.

Dearest Jesus, the deserts of my life are dry and uncomfortable. In those deserts, I long for your "Living Waters". I often try to quench my thirsting with other things; wealth, power, and prestige. They never satisfy, but how quickly I can turn to them for a quick fix for my thirsting. Jesus, thank you for the desert experiences of my life for they have taught me to search more ardently and fervently for your Living Waters.

"IT IS FINISHED."

He cries out, KALAH. It is finished. It is Passover. He is the Lamb who has been brought to be slaughtered. He has not run or cried out during this time of agony. I see that He is the sacrificial lamb. But He cries out the words of the High Priest when the last lamb is slaughtered on Passover. There has never been anything like this. I scarce can take it in. He is our sacrifice and He is our High Priest. My head reels, but my heart knows a peace and calm indescribable.

Jesus, with ears of faith I hear your words, "It is Finished." Like a runner who has crossed the finish line can declare His victory, so too you declare the victory. You, the sacrificial lamb, have paid the price. You, who in your obedience to the Father's will, have handed yourself over to the plan for your life. To do the Father's will was always your choice. Jesus, I desire to do the Father's will, but often I am not ready to pay the full price. Help me to say "yes" to the plan for my life. Help me to trust the Father as you did.

"FATHER, INTO YOUR HANDS I COMMEND MY SPIRIT."

Jesus knew the scriptures. Once more He is quoting our Psalms. The Word says, "Into your hands I commend my spirit; you will redeem me, O Lord, O faithful God." Further on it continues, "Let your face shine upon your servant; save me in your kindness. O Lord, let me not be put to shame, for I call upon you." The Psalm ends, "Take courage and be stouthearted, all you who hope in the Lord." This man Jesus has such faith in Yaweh. He believes in the Resurrection of the dead or He would never pray such a prayer. Look! His Spirit leaves!

The Last Seven Words

as heard by

Veronica

To some I am of such little importance few call me by name. Before that day, humility had cloaked my identity. I truly had no intention of being helpful or to stand out. I was just a by-stander. But now, some know me because of something that happened to me that day, something I was compelled to be a part of. I am Veronica.

I am speaking of the day that the man, Jesus, was crucified. I watched it all. I didn't know Him. I had heard of Him and I heard of these terrible events, so I decided to follow Him up the hill. I could never have dreamt how those few hours would change my life.

As He was carrying His cross, I could not understand what He had done wrong. I did not understand why they were torturing Him so. From what I had seen of His life, He had only helped people; He had only preached goodness and love. This cruelty didn't make any sense to me.

As I watched Him something began to stir in my heart. I had not yet decided if I was a follower of Jesus, but I was curious, and I knew that He was a good man. But what compelled me to follow Him up the hill? What made me feel such compassion?

I hurried further up the hill past Him and pushed my way through the crowd to get a better look. For some reason, I just had to see His face. I saw Him fall on the hard earth beneath the heavy cross, and the soldiers began to beat Him. I couldn't understand why they were so cruel. Couldn't they see He was suffering already? He was so weak, they forced a man to help Him carry the cross. I could see the man—Simon they called Him—was reluctant, but he obeyed. As Simon shouldered the cross, Jesus looked at him with gratitude and such love. How could He feel love amid all this pain?

As I was watching His face, suddenly He was crouched before me. I didn't realize that the people around me had backed away to let Him pass. I had been transfixed in my place watching this man. The soldiers started to yell at me, telling me to get out of the way, but His eyes were so kind, so soft, so full of love. I suddenly heard a voice in my heart, something I had heard before "Amen, I say to you, whatever you did for one of these least brothers of mine, you did for me." But what could I do?

I made up my mind. Instead of backing into the crowd, I stepped forward, pulled out a linen cloth, knelt before Him, and wiped His face. My hands caressed His brow, His cheek, His chin. His gaze held mine and in that moment nothing mattered but the love I knew in my heart.

I could hear gasps behind me, and suddenly the soldier's hands were on me pushing me backwards. I snatched the cloth and tucked it away as I was shoved into the crowd. But I did not go home. I followed Him up to the top of Golgotha, the place of the skull.

I watched them as they stripped Him of His clothing, laughing as they nailed Him to the cross. It was painful to watch, but for some reason, I could not take my eyes from this man. I thought it was over, that He would die in pain and silence, but as I stood there, riveted, He began to speak.

"FATHER, FORGIVE THEM. THEY KNOW NOT WHAT THEY DO."

Forgive them? I was confused. He was being treated with such cruelty, not only from the Romans, but religious leaders and the Jews, His own people. I didn't understand their cruelty at all, and I certainly didn't understand how Jesus could forgive them.

And who is this Father He is speaking to? I was filled with questions. But the question that disturbed me the most was, "why should He forgive them?" I don't think I could forgive like that. They are making a sport of killing this man, Jesus. They are showing no mercy. The effort it took to speak these words convinces me He means it, but why would He do it? It only further solidified my belief in His innocence, in His kindness and love.

"THIS DAY YOU WILL BE WITH ME IN PARADISE."

As I was still pondering forgiveness, He spoke again. There was a man on either side of Him, also being crucified. From their conversation I surmised that they were both criminals. One clearly believed that Jesus was "The Messiah." I know that I have felt that way before. Both criminals admitted they have done wrong. This man Jesus had done no wrong. "This day you will be with me in Paradise." Could He really be the Messiah? Only the Messiah could promise Paradise.

I know that when our first parents disobeyed they were cast out of Paradise. Jesus now promised a criminal Paradise. My heart, still burning from the time I comforted Him, tells me this is true. He must be the Messiah.

"WOMAN, BEHOLD YOUR SON. SON, BEHOLD YOUR MOTHER."

From where I had been standing I could see this woman and the man next to her. Her eyes never left Jesus. I knew she was His mother. Now that I look at her, I remember her eyes, full of love mingled with sorrow had been on me as I had wiped His brow. How much she must suffer seeing her son like this. The man at her side seemed overwhelmed by Jesus' words, as if no greater gift could have been given him. Clearly, He looked at her with love.

Love. There it was again. This whole scene kept me there because I felt such love. I was standing before men being crucified and all I felt was love. This man Jesus speaks of forgiveness, forgiveness even back to our parents Adam and Eve, and clearly, He cares deeply for this woman and the man standing next to her. The love is tangible. Love is what compelled me to step out of the crowd and wipe His face before the soldiers' whips and the crowd's jeers. I had never felt love like this.

"MY GOD, MY GOD, WHY HAVE YOU FORSAKEN ME?"

As I was basking in this experience of love, my mind was trying to comprehend what was happening. My heart told me that Jesus is the Messiah, the one all of Israel is waiting for.

Slowly with tremendous effort He raised up again to speak. He looked so tired, so exhausted. His "words" define His situation. He was feeling forsaken, abandoned, desolate, cut off from His God. I recognized His words "My God, my God why have you forsaken me?" from Psalm 22, the psalm of an innocent man. Suddenly, I knew with all my heart. He is the fulfillment of the Scriptures. He truly is the Messiah! My heart was breaking to hear these words coming from His heart.

God why must He go through such suffering? I can't help Him. I can't take Him down from this cross. I can't bind up His wounds. I tried to comfort Him, but what I did seems so small. What else can I do? What else can you do?

"I THIRST."

As I was looking at Him with a breaking heart, a bystander ran to get a sponge. He soaked it in some wine the soldiers had brought for themselves, put the sponge on a reed and raised it to Jesus' lips. Jesus took the wine. As He sipped on the sponge His eyes met the bystander's. I saw that same look of unending love He had given me. This "little gesture" of comfort had been multiplied. I saw that this bystander and I were now connected in God's love. Our kindness had been small, but we had loved Jesus in the way that we knew how. I was speechless, overwhelmed with gratitude. Christ had allowed us to comfort Him.

Jesus, I remember seeing you that day when you said, "And whoever gives only a cup of cold water to one of these little ones to drink because he is a disciple—amen, I say to you, he will surely not lose His reward." Now I know what that means. I am so grateful that I could comfort you with just my cloth to wipe your face. I want to serve you always. Your love is irresistible. Thank you for loving me. Thank you for allowing me to comfort you in your suffering. Thank you!

"IT IS FINISHED."

Finished? What does He mean by finished? No sooner than I had thought my question, an answer popped into my heart. He is the Messiah, the sacrificial lamb, the fulfillment of the Scriptures. His work is finished in this body. He is the unblemished lamb, the perfect sacrifice. The Passover is finished. And yet, everything is just beginning.

I remembered that Jesus continually preached about a Kingdom, a Kingdom of His Father's. It is a Kingdom of love. Love for God, His Father, is what this Kingdom is about. But it is also about love for all people. We know the Kingdom comes when we love each other. When we offer a cup of blessing to our brother or sister in need we are bringing in His kingdom. The Kingdom comes in small and large expressions of love. His work was finished, when He saw the Kingdom come in my "little gesture" of love. What a privilege to serve in the Kingdom.

"FATHER, INTO YOUR HANDS I COMMEND MY SPIRIT."

As the darkness descended in the brightest time of the day, Jesus hung on His cross. Suddenly, in renewed vigor and strength, Jesus raised himself up on the cross. In a shout of victory he called out, "Father into your hands I commend my Spirit." His body may have been weakened, but His Spirit soared. There was victory in His voice. He bowed His head and died. The earth shook; the temple veil tore in half and light came back upon the earth. No longer were we separated from God's presence on Earth. The veil had been destroyed. His work was done. His mission accomplished.

I had been anonymous before the death of this man Jesus on the cross. But the love in His eyes compelled me to reach out to Him. His words changed my life forever. I now understand and believe in His Father's kingdom. I know my actions, no matter how small, do have meaning and are seen and received with love by the Father. I beg you to hear His words. Do not feel that you cannot make a difference. No matter how small your act of love, God will magnify it for His kingdom.

The Last Seven Words

as heard by

The Crucifier

I was there that Friday morning. It was my job to be there. Many times I had climbed the hill of Calvary. This day didn't seem any different than any other day. I had heard that there would be three of them that day. I had already finished doing my job for two of them when I heard this commotion. I looked down the hill and I could see this man carrying His cross. Someone was behind Him making the load easier. There were a few people walking at a distance behind these two. What a sight He was. He was covered in blood from a scourging. He must have been quite a trouble maker, only the worst criminals get the services of my job. There was even a crown of thorns on His head. I wondered who this man was, although it wouldn't make any difference. I had a job to do and I did it.

Now, many may think it isn't much of a job, but I am skilled at what I do. It took training to insure there would be no mistakes in my placement. Many might think I don't have a heart, but I do. I was only doing my job. I had to learn to concentrate on my job and not on the person. Some were easier than others. I didn't know anything about this man. When I finished my job, I was given a message to hang above His head. It said, "This is Jesus, King of the Jews". I didn't pay much attention to the Jews. I didn't know their God. I was a pagan. Like I said, I was only doing my job. I could have cared less about this man. It was my job to crucify Him.

By the way, you won't find my name in the scriptures. Only your heart will tell you who I am. My name is **Everyone**. I am **Everyone**. I am the one who crucified Jesus. This Jesus was unlike anyone else I had nailed to the cross. He spoke a few times as He hung there. They were Words that I couldn't understand at the time, but they touched my heart. It wasn't until a Jewish Feast Day a few weeks later that I understood. It was Pentecost, early in the morning, and I was saved by this same man I had crucified. Now, His Words on the Cross make sense. I savor those words and love to tell **Everyone** what I heard that day on Calvary.

"FATHER, FORGIVE THEM. THEY KNOW NOT WHAT THEY DO."

You can't imagine the strength it takes for someone to rise up on the cross when their lungs are full of air, and then choose to speak. But that wasn't what got to me. I swear He looked at me when He said those words. He was forgiving me for doing my job. He looked with compassion. Something I never had for Him when I nailed Him on that cross. Why would this man, Jesus, want to forgive me? I wonder who His Father is. I wanted to run. I was only doing my job. It never mattered to me how I hurt people. They were criminals. They were less than me. Besides, someone has to do what needs to be done. Forgiveness complicates life when you are doing your job.

Lord, how often do I crucify people by my words and my actions? Do I offer the same excuse, "I'm only doing my job"? Forgiveness is a word that seldom wants to cross my lips, when I am busy doing my work, my will. Forgiveness makes me realize my responsibility to the other. Forgiveness comes from a heart that loves.

"THIS DAY YOU'LL BE WITH ME IN PARADISE."

This Jesus spoke forgiveness and now He is offering paradise to a criminal. Paradise, what is paradise? That criminal seems to know Jesus is not guilty of His charges. What have I done? Have I crucified an innocent man? This is complicated. If Jesus is innocent, then surely I am guilty. Those thoughts made me feel uncomfortable. After all I was only doing my job. What difference does it make who is innocent and who is guilty? Besides, He is dying. How can He promise anything? Who can obtain Paradise from a dying man?

When my eyes were opened, I realized that Jesus is innocent and I am a sinner. Jesus offers me new life. My life can begin anew. Jesus, you call me to forgiveness. You show me my guilt just as you show me forgiveness. It is a choice I must make. Excuses are no longer valid. Life anew is living in Paradise. Paradise is that place where there is no guilt. Paradise is that place where doing the will of Jesus and depending on Him is my choice.

"WOMAN, BEHOLD YOUR SON, SON BEHOLD YOUR MOTHER."

There was this woman standing by His cross. She couldn't keep her eyes off of Him. I'm not a very sensitive person. I usually can avoid my feelings. I took a quick look at her when He spoke and I was so sorry I did. Life is hard. Why did she bother to come to this hill? She'd have been better off to avoid all of this. Who wants to see a man die, especially your son? I didn't know who the man was, but He obviously knew this woman. Some people might think crucifying someone is hard to do, but it was more difficult for me to see those looks of love between them.

After Pentecost, I learned that the woman was indeed His mother. Her name is Mary. They say the man was the Beloved Disciple. She was with that group that morning of Pentecost. They apparently were praying for the Holy Spirit to come as Jesus had promised. I can tell you the Spirit came. Since they told me the "Good News" and I received that Spirit, I know I am just like that man, a Beloved Disciple. I have even gotten to know Mary. She is a remarkable woman.

"MY GOD, MY GOD WHY HAVE YOU FORSAKEN ME?"

Most men I have crucified never call out to God, rather, they curse God as if it is His fault for their circumstances. I didn't pay much attention to religion. I wasn't sure what I believed about God. When you don't believe, it is difficult to think of anyone calling out to God. After I heard these last words of Jesus, I began to think about a God. Who is God? Why should I want Him in my life? I began to feel forsaken. I didn't know God and I didn't know where to look for Him. I wasn't sure if I could find Him.

That all changed at Pentecost. On Pentecost the whole town was afire. People were talking about Jesus. They told me He rose from the dead. They had seen Him afterwards. They said He had sent the promised Holy Spirit. They told me how to find God. They said to repent and believe the Good News. God wants to be found. Jesus is willing to show us the Way.

"I THIRST."

There is nothing unusual about Him crying out that He thirst. Crucifixion is a horrible way to die. You bleed from your wounds and that causes you to be thirsty. This man, Jesus, was scourged before His crucifixion and He had lost much of His blood. Then there was that crown of thorns on His head. Just looking at Him, I knew He would be thirsting. He was different though because He didn't want the drugged wine we offered Him when He was first crucified. Most of them being crucified beg for it. When He cried out in His thirst some fellow ran up with common wine and He drank it from the sponge offered on a branch of hyssop. Guess He finally was thirsty enough to drink.

After I heard the Good News I discovered how wrong I was about that word. He was really saying He was thirsting for my soul. I had stood there and heard His word, but never imagined it was me He was thirsting for. My heart and my understanding were so closed that even in hearing I never heard. Now I know He thirsts for **Everyone**. He went through His crucifixion for **Everyone**. I know that now. Jesus thirsts for you too.

"IT IS FINISHED."

His words are like riddles to understand when your heart is closed. When I heard those words, I knew He was finished. There is no hope when you are being crucified. Blood was flowing, air was trapped in His lungs, and His tendons are ripped apart and sing a song of agony. It is a cruel finish. Nervously, I laughed when I heard those words. He certainly was coming to His end, thanks to my ability to do my job. I never felt remorse before. What is this man doing to my mind? He is getting under my skin and I don't like it. I am feeling like it is my fault He had to die. He is the criminal, not me. What foolishness I am thinking.

After Pentecost, I knew it was not foolishness. He had died for my sins. He died for **Everyone's** sins. It was finished. There was nothing else He could do. He took **Everyone's** sins and died. Now I believe that Jesus rose from the dead. I believe Jesus ascended to His Father. I believe my sins are forgiven. I believe the price was paid for **Everyone.** Jesus isn't the sinner. **Everyone** is the sinner. But in Jesus' death, sin has been forgiven. On that cross Jesus defeated sin.

"FATHER, INTO YOUR HANDS I COMMEND MY SPIRIT."

This was His last word. I would have expected He would barely have whispered this last word. But instead, He shouted it with a strength I can't describe. It was like a shout of victory. What is the victory in dying? Why would you say such a thing at a time like this? Again, who is this Father He keeps talking to? Truthfully, I was glad it was over. This man really disturbed me. I just came to Calvary to do my job. I was not a novice. I was well trained for my job. Usually, I could walk down the hill after my job was finished and not think about it again. Not that day. Even nature seemed to be with this man. The sky had darkened, thunder clapped at His death, and the earth literally shook under our feet. How could anyone not think about the day that this Jesus, King of the Jews, was crucified? Those Seven Last Words were written on my heart that day. I didn't know where to go or what to do with them.

I truly didn't know what to do, until that day of Pentecost. They told me everything I needed to know. I heard it in my own language. They didn't have to tell me I was a sinner. I could see that I am a sinner. I could hear that I am a sinner. **Everyone** is a sinner! People listen to me! Jesus was a man whom God sent to us with miracles, wonders and signs as His credentials. Jesus was delivered up by the set purpose and plan of God. He even made use of me, a pagan, to crucify and kill Him. God raised Him up, for it was impossible that death should keep its hold on him. I am His witness. Jesus is exalted at God's right hand. Jesus received the promised Holy Spirit. He then poured this Spirit out on us. Therefore let **Everyone** know beyond any doubt that, He whom we crucified, is our Lord and Savior, Jesus Christ.

The Last Seven Words

as heard by

A Roman Soldier

Sometimes we marvel at what life can bring to us so unexpectedly. I am an ordinary soldier in the Roman Army. One day my assignment was to accompany this person to be crucified. He was a beaten man. He had been flogged and His skin was ripped and bleeding. He had a cap of thorns upon His head. Amazingly, He was still alive. But I wondered for how long. Going to the hill wasn't easy for Him, but He made it.

We did our work and nailed Him to the cross. When you know how to do it, it doesn't take much time. He was a strange man. He never uttered a word when the nails went in. He wouldn't even take the drink we offered Him. I wondered what His story was.

Of course, we had stripped Him of His clothes before we hung Him. Those clothes were bloody, but still worthwhile. We each took what we wanted. There was this tunic woven in one piece from top to bottom which we all wanted. It was too valuable to be torn, so we decided to throw dice for it. It was my lucky day. The roll of the dice proclaimed me as the winner of His robe. Little did I realize what a prize I had won. Because of that robe, my life has never been the same. All I knew then was I had His robe and the others didn't. I was a Roman soldier and knew so little about this occupied land of the Jews. All I knew was this man was a Jew and His own people had wanted Him crucified. Pilate had a sign hung on His cross which read "Jesus the Nazorean, King of the Jews". It didn't matter. I had their King's Robe. I'd won it fair and square. You can't imagine what the next few hours were like. Jesus pulled himself up on the cross seven times to speak. This dying man spoke seven times. His words, though I didn't fully comprehend their meaning then, touched my heart like fire. I had His Robe, but He had my heart.

"FATHER, FORGIVE THEM. THEY KNOW NOT WHAT THEY DO."

I swear He was looking at me when He said those words. His words made me fearful. I was just doing my job. I know what I am doing. I am a good soldier. I do what my superiors tell me to do. If I want to please my boss, I better do as He says. Who does this Jesus think He is suggesting that I am doing something wrong? You learn early in this world how to please people so life is a little easier for you. If I don't look out for myself, who will look out for me? Why would He want to forgive me, I never even say I am sorry? No one has ever forgiven me. Those are strange words. The man is dying, why is He concerned with forgiveness? Why with your last breath would you ever offer forgiveness? Doesn't sound like a king to me?

Lord, I am just like the soldier. Forgiveness is difficult. Saying I am sorry hurts my pride. Hearing you say that I am forgiven sometimes is difficult for me to believe. Jesus, help me to forgive like you forgive.

"THIS DAY YOU WILL BE WITH ME IN PARADISE."

Is He crazy? He is hanging on a cross and He is promising that man beside him Paradise. He is going to be dead soon. There is no Paradise. When you die, it is over. He sounds crazy, but my heart wants to believe it is true. Could there be a Paradise?

Jesus, my faith tells me there is Paradise. We call it Paradise, that place where you and your Father dwell. That thief beside you on His cross repented. Repentance leads us to where you and the Father are. You aren't crazy. You just love so completely that our repentance can quickly bring us back into Paradise with you. Lord, I want to repent of everything that keeps me from receiving all the love you want to give me. This day I want to be in Paradise with you.

"WOMAN, BEHOLD YOUR SON. SON, BEHOLD YOUR MOTHER."

I saw this woman while walking the way of the cross. I knew she knew Him by the looks that passed between them. Most women would avoid a crucifixion, but she and a few other women stayed the entire time. I wondered who that man next to her was. Guess Jesus didn't want that woman to be alone. I guess a mother would stay with her son if she didn't have anyone else. Why did Jesus call her woman instead of Mother? That man, Jesus, speaks in riddles.

Jesus sometimes I wonder about my friends who talk so much about Mary, your mother. I know she is your mother, but I don't know her very well. Jesus, you are the important one in my life. Jesus, your words challenge me. Do you really mean for Mary to be my Mother too? I don't understand. Help me to see the gift of your mother in my life.

"MY GOD, MY GOD, WHY HAVE YOU FORSAKEN ME?"

That is what I expected from a man being crucified. They always cry out when they see there is no hope. Jesus must have been feeling hopeless. Why wouldn't He feel that way? He is naked, condemned and now He has given His mother away. I wonder who His god is. We Romans have many gods. I wonder who His favorite god is. No god can save Him now. Why would you pray anyway? No one is listening.

Jesus, many days I feel like no one is listening to me. I pray and pray and nothing changes. I truly feel forsaken, so alone. I might not be on a cross, but it feels like an invisible cross of suffering. No one seems to understand, not even me. I just know I feel hopeless and forsaken, all alone. Where are you when I need you?

"I THIRST."

Of course, He is thirsty. They all get thirsty. It must be because He has lost so much blood. I put some wine on a hyssop branch and held it up to Him. He took it, but the look He gave me made my heart do funny things. Who is this man? Why do His looks touch my heart like that? This has never happened to me before. I felt like I could answer His thirst. This is crazy. What is happening to me?

Jesus, sometimes I get thirsty too. I want answers. I want understanding. I want knowledge. I want an experience of you. I want to believe you are real, but sometimes I have my doubts. I hear people talk about you as if you are their best friend and I get jealous. Why can't I know you like they do? I am thirsty!

"IT IS FINISHED."

What is finished? This man is so peculiar. He is different than any man I have crucified. Does He know His end is imminent? We all know it is. Why spend the energy to tell us what we already know? He is going to die. We all die, some easier than others. What is so special about His death? Why does He insist on telling us it is finished?

Jesus, I wonder what my last words will be before I die. Will I believe my life is ending? Will I think I still have things to do? Things I have failed to do or people I need to make peace with? Will I fight death in fear of my future? What do I think about the future? What does, "It is finished" mean to me?

"FATHER, INTO YOUR HANDS I COMMEND MY SPIRIT."

He shouted like He was victorious. Who is His Father that He is talking to? At least it is His spirit He is giving to the Father. Who would want this bruised, beaten, bloody body? This man is so strange. Jesus said these words and died.

I walked away from this crucifixion carrying His Robe. But I carried so much more. His words continued to play in my heart and my head. Weeks passed by, and I still had no understanding of these events. All I had was His Robe. I heard the gossip on the streets that said Jesus had risen, but I didn't believe it. I saw the man die. I saw the wound in His heart from the lance. He couldn't have risen.

But that is not the end of my story. I was out on the street some many days later, when I happened on that man who Jesus talked to on the cross. You know that man He gave His mother to. I recognized Him. He was standing in the square talking about this Jesus. He seemed to have an inner fire in Him. Someone said it was because of what happened to Him on Pentecost. The whole town was talking about this event. These followers of Jesus had an experience that changed their lives.

He told me Jesus was the Son of God. Not one of the Roman gods, but the God who had created everything. Jesus is the God above all gods. This Jesus worked signs and wonders while He walked this earth. The woman was Mary, His mother and mine too. Mary conceived Jesus by the Holy Spirit. The same Holy Spirit these followers had received on Pentecost. He said Jesus died for my sins. That Jesus rose again and they all had seen Him. That He had ascended into heaven and they had seen Him go up. He told me all I had to do was repent of my old ways, my sinful ways, and believe the Good News about Jesus.

I did repent. I believe the Good News. I had a robe that belonged to a man crucified. I won it in a dice game. Now I have a Robe of Righteousness that comes from Jesus. I am clothed in His love and His mercy. He finished sin and death on His cross. His Spirit now lives in me. His Robe is so precious!

The Last Seven Words

as heard by

Peter

You might not want to believe it, but I was there that day that Jesus died. I watched it all; at a distance, of course. My name is Peter! Peter means ROCK, someone strong in spirit. I'm sure you've heard about me and my boasting. I thought I was strong in spirit, until I was faced with the cross. The cross has a way of making us tremble. The cross brings us awareness of those dark hidden places within us. When I said, "Even though all should have their faith shaken, mine will not be". I did not know the truth of my humanity. I did not know my own human weakness. The cross made me recognize and admit my own poverty and darkness. It is those dark parts of ourselves which we so often fear and deny that hold the key to our conversion.

Coming from darkness to light is a journey. Jesus really knows us better than we know ourselves. It was only after His death, that I could take comfort in the knowledge that Jesus knew I would deny Him before it happened. Jesus launched me on a journey of self discovery through His sufferings on the cross. When faced with the burden of the cross, I wondered why I got involved in a way of life that demanded so much. We Christians want to follow Jesus, but we are tempted to do it "at a distance".

But remember, it is a journey. When I stood a distance from the cross and heard those Seven Last Words, I was reluctant to acknowledge I knew Him. The Beloved Disciple and Mary and a few other folks could stand right at the foot of the cross. I was too ashamed, bewildered at the new truth I'd learned about myself, to choose a front row position. I kept a distance between us.

Our Christian life is a journey. It is a journey from birth to death to new life in the Spirit. The cross and the Seven Last Words of Jesus would make no sense if that were all there was. Granted there was that period of time lying in the tomb; dead to the old, but not yet risen to the new. There was also that time after the Resurrection. I knew that He had risen, but the fullness of the Spirit He had promised had not come. His words can always be trusted and on Pentecost a new power came into my life, just as He had promised. All was changed for me. I no longer desired to follow "at a distance". I bravely want to tell the whole world the "Good News". Telling people of every race and nationality about Jesus Christ; crucified on a cross, risen from the dead and coming again in glory is what I desire to proclaim forever.

"FATHER, FORGIVE THEM. THEY KNOW NOT WHAT THEY DO."

Do you hear Him? He is talking to me. Is He talking to you? I didn't know I'd deny Him. I couldn't believe that was truth about me. I thought I knew myself. I loved Him! You don't deny that which you love. Or do you? My love has limits. Sometimes love is too costly. It will cost me my status, my position, my opinion of myself and the opinions of others. Jesus once told me that I had to forgive seventy times seven times. There are just some things that are too hard to forgive. Like when I fail, when I fall off that throne I've erected for myself. Forgiving me and forgiving others isn't easy. It takes humility to say, "I'm sorry, forgive me". Jesus knows how difficult it is for us, but He shows us it is possible to forgive in the very worst of situations.

Jesus, help me learn to forgive as you did.

"THIS DAY YOU WILL BE WITH ME IN PARADISE."

Can you believe it? Jesus offers a criminal Paradise as He hangs on the cross. The doors of Paradise were closed with the sin of our father Adam. It was revealed to me that Jesus was the Messiah, the Son of the living God. I had come to believe, I was convinced that Jesus was God's holy one. What a leap of faith to believe that Jesus could offer Paradise, and offer it to a common criminal. The criminal knew His sinfulness. He knew He deserved punishment. He only asked Jesus to remember him when Jesus entered into His reign. Jesus assured the criminal that this day He would be with Him in Paradise. I immediately knew that Jesus was saying the same thing to me. You see, you just have to acknowledge your sinfulness and seek His mercy and He will give you Paradise.

Jesus, help me to realize that when I'm living in a state of grace, I'm already living in Paradise.

"WOMAN, BEHOLD YOUR SON. SON, BEHOLD YOUR MOTHER."

That woman is His mother, Mary. She is a special woman. She never stands at a distance. Over the years I was with Jesus, I got to know her. There truly is uniqueness about their relationship. She isn't impulsive like me. She knows how to ponder and is truly open to the Spirit of God. Some folks think that Jesus was just giving Mary to John, but I believe Jesus wants me to take her into my care, too. I also believe Jesus wants you to take her into your care. She never takes honor from her Son, but rather is open to His glory.

Holy Mother, make your presence known to all disciples.

"MY GOD, MY GOD, WHY HAVE YOU FORSAKEN ME?"

Oh, how Jesus loved the scriptures. He knew them so well. Often times, He taught us things we'd never observed in the Holy Words. He loved the 22nd Psalm and was fond of reciting it to us. Now I see why. It is talking about Him. Look, they have pierced His hands and His feet. You can count all His bones as

He hangs on the cross. They did cast lots for His garments. The beginning of that Psalm is so depressing It is all about suffering, His suffering. No wonder He is praying those words. Yet the Psalm ends with praising. It calls the Israelites and all of humankind to praise what God has done in His suffering Servant.

Jesus, help me to belong to the people of praise, a people who know the gift of the Suffering Servant.

"I THIRST."

Jesus once said to the Samaritan woman, "Whoever drinks the water I give him will never be thirsty; no, the water I give shall become a fountain within him, leaping up to provide eternal life." I understand with new understanding. Jesus is thirsting for my faith. In return, He promises to allow me to drink of the Holy Spirit in satisfying abundance. I can almost hear Him saying, "I want to give living water to every thirsty soul. There are people who are thirsting for true life. Go to all people. I want to pour out my living water for them. They are thirsty; they are dying. Give them the true living waters of the Holy Spirit. I am commissioning you. The Church is to give the living waters to those who are dying of thirst."

Jesus, help me to quench your thirst.

"IT IS FINISHED."

My Jewish brother and Messiah knew the words of the High Priest on Passover. When the last sacrifice had been offered; the High Priest cries out, "It is finished." Our Savior is telling us that the sacrifice is completed. He offered himself for our sins. There is no need for further sacrifice. Can you believe it? He took our sins on the cross. He paid the price for our transgressions. There is nothing more to offer. It is finished. How dare we not accept this precious gift of His? He knows our sinful, human flesh, our denials, our desire to distance ourselves from the cross of suffering and He offers himself as our Pascal lamb.

Jesus, I shout my song of praise for the gift you offer to us!

"FATHER, INTO YOUR HANDS I COMMEND MY SPIRIT."

Once Jesus said, "Doing the will of Him who sent me and bringing His work to completion is my food." Jesus brought His work to completion on the cross. It was finished. There was no more work to do. Truly no one took His life. He willingly offered it to His God and Father for you and me. There is no greater love than this: to lay down one's life for one's friends. And we are His friends if we do what He commands us. So open your hearts to Jesus. Allow Him to give you the courage to speak His name to those who are close to you and the generosity to share His love with those who are far away. Pray that every person throughout the world be invited to know and love Jesus as their Savior and Redeemer. May we all come to know His love. May we never be content when we are at a distance from His cross.

The Last Seven Words

as heard by

An Anonymous By-Stander

To some I am of such little importance no one calls me by name. Humility would cloak my identity. Not a self imposed humility, but rather humility imposed on me. I truly had no intention of being helpful, a do-gooder. I was just a **by-stander**. It just happened; as I watched the events of that day unfold. I am speaking of the day that the man, Jesus, was crucified. I watched it all. I didn't know Him. I just happened to be there and I stopped to watch. I could never have dreamt how those few hours would change my life. He spoke Seven Times, and those words changed my life forever.

I have had time to reflect on my experience. I would desire to remain anonymous as I tell you what happened to me on that day. That man, Jesus, spoke seven times while He hung on the cross. I believe it is His words that held me there that day. The poor fellow obviously had been scourged before He got to that place. His body was badly beaten. Frankly, I wondered how He had survived His abuse. But it was so clear that He had "words" He wanted to speak as He hung there. It took tremendous effort for Him to speak. But speak He did. His words were clear, concise and went into your heart. I had never heard anyone speak like this. There was time between His words to ponder, think and digest what I heard. Now as I look back, I realize how my heart was being changed, little by little. His "words" were powerful. They were life changing.

The soldiers offered Him a drink of wine flavored with gall when He got to Golgotha, but He refused it. He had to be thirsty, but He wanted no part of that drugged wine. Then they nailed Him to the cross. I can still hear the sharp crack of the hammer as the nails pierced His skin. I was ready to leave then, but as I watched, He pulled himself up on the cross and He spoke the first time— "

"FATHER, FORGIVE THEM. THEY KNOW NOT WHAT THEY DO."

Who is this Man? Forgive them. What could anyone do that would deserve such cruel treatment? It was not just Romans mocking Him. There appeared to be religious leaders as well. What did He do to them? Why would Romans and Jews want this vengeance? There was a sign above His head. It read, "This is Jesus, King of the Jews". Why would the Romans care about this man if He is Jewish? The Jews haven't had a king for a long time. Who is this man that brought out such hatred in these people? Why would He choose to forgive them? Who is this Father He is speaking to? Poor fellow, he must be out of His mind. But why would you crucify someone whose mind is not right?

I am filled with questions. But the question that disturbed me the most was, "why would He forgive them?" Let me tell you, I wouldn't be so quick to forgive under these circumstances. They are making a sport of killing this man, Jesus. They are showing no mercy. Although they did offer Him that drugged wine which He refused. Nevertheless, I certainly would not be offering forgiveness.

The effort it took to speak these words convinces me He means it, but why would He do it? Who is this man? Who is this Father?

"THIS DAY YOU WILL BE WITH ME IN PARADISE"

As I was still mulling over that forgiveness word, He spoke again. There was a man on either side of Him, also being crucified. From their conversation I surmised that they were both criminals. They seem to think this fellow is "The Messiah". They admit they have done wrong. This man Jesus, the one criminal maintains has done no wrong. In fact, it is in His asking Jesus to remember him when He enters His reign that prompts Jesus word, "This day you will be with me in Paradise." Clearly, this man Jesus must think He is a Messiah if He goes to all the effort to promise such a thing. Maybe this man really is out of His mind. Who could promise Paradise?

I know that when our first parents disobeyed they were cast out of Paradise. This man Jesus has promised a criminal Paradise. It is so strange. My mind says, "How can He promise such a thing?" Yet my heart tells me this is true. Am I being fooled by this man, Jesus? Can he really promise him or me Paradise?

"WOMAN, BEHOLD YOUR SON. SON, BEHOLD YOUR MOTHER."

From where I had been standing I could see this woman and the man next to her. Her eyes never left Jesus. I had thought she might be His mother. I really had wanted to go to her and comfort her, but I was fearful. Besides where would such a desire come from? Better not to get involved. The man at her side seemed overwhelmed by these words, as if no greater gift could have been given Him. Clearly, He looked at her with love.

That's when it hit me. This whole scene keeps me here because I feel such love. I'm standing before men being crucified and all I feel is love. This man Jesus speaks of forgiveness, forgiveness even back to our parents Adam and Eve, and clearly He cares deeply for this woman and the man standing next to her. The love is tangible. I feel it. I have never felt love like this.

"MY GOD, MY GOD, WHY HAVE YOU FORSAKEN ME?"

As I was basking in this experience of love, my mind was trying to comprehend what was happening. Who is this man? Who is this Jesus? Is He the Messiah? I know all of Israel is waiting for a Messiah. Slowly with tremendous effort He rose up again to speak. He looked so tired, so exhausted. His "words" define His situation. He was feeling forsaken, abandoned, desolate, cut off from His God. My heart was breaking to hear this word coming from His heart.

I don't know this man, but I feel such compassion for Him. God, why aren't you there for Him? I can't help Him. I can't take Him down from this cross. I can't bind up His wounds. I can't comfort Him. There is nothing I can do to show comfort or compassion to my new found love. How do you comfort someone who is in such a situation?

"I THIRST."

Hardly, had I heard this word and I immediately found myself running to get a sponge. I soaked the sponge in some wine the soldiers had brought for themselves, put the sponge on a reed and raised it up to His lips. Jesus took the wine. As He sipped on the sponge His eyes met mine. I couldn't take my eyes from Him. This "little gesture" of comfort made my heart so happy. I know it wasn't much, but I had reached out to Him. I loved Him back from the love He had placed in my heart. I was speechless, overwhelmed with gratitude. Somehow I had wanted to comfort Him. I was able to give Him something for His thirst. He didn't refuse me. He seemed eager to accept my "little gift".

Suddenly, I heard these words in my heart—"I promise you that whoever gives a cup of cold water to one of these lowly ones because He is my disciple will not want for His reward." Lord Jesus, what are you saying to my heart? I am so grateful that I could give you that wine. I would want to serve you always. Your love is irresistible. Thank you for softening my heart. Thank you for allowing me to give you a drink in your thirst. Thank you!

"IT IS FINISHED."

Again, His "word" made no sense to me. What was finished? No sooner than I had thought my question, an answer popped into my heart. "I solemnly assure you, I will drink of the fruit of the vine when I drink it new in the reign of God." I didn't understand. I had to think about this answer I had received in my heart. Jesus spoke clearly, but I needed time to ponder this word, "It is finished".

What I learned about this man Jesus was that He continually preached about a Kingdom, a Kingdom of His Father's. It is a Kingdom of love. Love for God, His Father, is what this Kingdom is about. But it is also about love for all people. We know the Kingdom comes when we love each other. When we offer a cup of blessing to our brother or sister in need we are bringing in His kingdom. The Kingdom comes in small and large expressions of love. His work was finished, when He saw the Kingdom come in my "little gesture" of love. What a privilege to serve in the Kingdom..

"FATHER, INTO YOUR HANDS I COMMEND MY SPIRIT"

As the darkness had descended in the brightest time of the day, Jesus hung on His cross. Suddenly, in renewed vigor and strength, Jesus raised himself up on the cross. In a shout of victory He called out, "Father into your hands I commend my Spirit." His body may have been weakened, but His Spirit soared. There was victory in His voice. He bowed His head and died. The earth shook; the temple veil tore in half and light came back upon the earth. His work was done. His mission accomplished.

I was merely an anonymous bystander at the death of this man Jesus on the cross. But His words changed my life forever. I had a cold, indifferent heart, lacking in love for myself or others. His words changed all of that. Serving another was not part of my life. I kept to myself and mostly took care of my needs. His words changed me. I never knew about His Father's Kingdom, but I do now. His words changed my understanding. Today I am no longer anonymous. I am proud to call myself a Christian, a follower of this man Jesus. I beg you to hear His words. Do not be content to be a by-stander, but rather become a follower of Jesus.

The Last Seven Words

as heard by

Mary of Magdala

The one reality that each of us shares as human beings is death. All of us will DIE. The when, where and how of death, we don't always know. But the reality of death, we do know. There will be a day when we take our last breath and die.

This is the reality of the man Jesus as He was dying. He spoke seven times from the cross, or His Seven Last Words. These words have been handed down over the centuries for our remembrance. So I invite you today to stop awhile and reflect on these words, as we remember the death of Jesus on the cross.

There is another reality we share, and that is that we have all sinned. Jesus did not sin, but He took our sins on himself on the cross. There was someone in Jesus' life that was a special lady. She was special because of what she did with her sin. She confessed her sin. She repented. She embraced forgiveness. She embraced her deliverance from sin. She is Mary of Magdala or Mary Magdalen. Mary was born in a town on the shore of the Sea of Galilee called Magdala. It is in the northern part of the Holy Land, a place where Jewish people mostly followed the Gentile ways and manners. Mary Magdalen is a saint who has a special title. She is called "the Penitent". She was sorry for having done wrong and was willing to atone for her sins. She stood at the foot of the cross with Mary, the mother of Jesus. Mary, that woman, who was conceived Immaculate. What a contrast these two women are, the Immaculate One and the Forgiven Sinner. Together they stand at the foot of the cross and listen to the words of Jesus in His death agony. The pain of seeing Him, whom their hearts love, touches both of their hearts.

Hear the words of Jesus as reflected on by Mary of Magdala. Hear the words from the ears of a repented sinner. "I can't believe it. I can't take it in. Jesus, my Jesus, what are they doing to you? It's not just. It is I who should be crucified. My sins were as scarlet. You are the sweetest, kindest, loving man I've ever known. And they hang you on a tree like a common criminal. You said this would happen, but I didn't believe you. I've only seen you doing good. You healed the sick. You set people free. You taught and spoke with such authority. You loved; you loved even me, a sinner. This is madness. This man is so special. I should know. He cast seven demons out of me."

Crucifixion is such a torture, especially to the lungs. Breath gets trapped in the lungs and cannot be expelled. Oh Jesus, how you suffer. —

"FATHER, FORGIVE THEM. THEY KNOW NOT WHAT THEY DO."

Forgive them. Jesus, you are forgiving them, just like you forgave me. I had seven demons cast from me. The sin I embraced was so deep and dark. My sin drove me to become less and less loving. It was horrible. I was doing my own thing, and I was being manipulated and enslaved into doing the devil's things. Darkness of sin became my light. I couldn't bear the light until you came into my life. You set me free when I turned to you. The darkness fled from me in the light of your love. No darkness can exist in your love. It has to go. Jesus, you spoke so often to us about forgiveness. You said all strife, all war, and all broken relationships come about because of a lack of forgiveness. You told me if I didn't forgive, I couldn't be forgiven. Jesus, you helped me to forgive them. You helped me to forgive myself. That was hard. I had to be around you for a while before I could really forgive myself.

Dear Jesus, hear my prayers for forgiveness. My brothers and sisters don't know what they are doing. Their sin has become such a part of them; they hardly recognize it as sin any more. There is so much strife, war, and broken relationships in their lives. Please, Jesus, remove it from them, as you took it from me when I asked for forgiveness. Jesus, it is difficult for us to initiate forgiveness. You helped me, help them. Jesus, you forgive them, help them forgive themselves. Help them to see you love the sinner, but not the sin.

"THIS DAY YOU WILL BE WITH ME IN PARADISE."

This day, Oh Jesus, I understand. Today! Today we can experience paradise. Isn't that irony? There is a "good" thief and a "bad" thief hanging on either side of you. All it took was an acknowledgment of His sins and you assure him that today he will be in paradise with you. Paradise, that's a safe place. It's the garden or the park connected to the royal residence. It's being in that safe place with you, Jesus. I know about paradise. I really couldn't explain it to everyone. It is something you have to experience. It is that safe place, where you are peaceful and contented. It is a place of calm and assurance that all is well.

Jesus, help them understand what you are offering them. You are offering them forgiveness for their sins, so that they can dwell in paradise with you. Just like me, they have to make a choice, accept forgiveness or reject it. You know, Jesus, at first my pride stood in the way. I didn't want to acknowledge my loneliness and separation from you. I pretended that everything was okay. But you saw through my pride. Your loving words broke down my resistance. Jesus, I wish everybody would have a chance to hear your words. Oh Jesus, I wish everybody could enjoy your paradise.

"WOMAN, BEHOLD YOUR SON. SON, BEHOLD YOUR MOTHER."

Jesus, I know Mary is special to you. I remember watching you looking at her. The looks that passed between you can't really be described. Everybody knows how much you love her. I've had a chance to get to know her, since I've been traveling along with you. When I am with her, it is so much like being with you. She seems to reflect you in such a special way. She never seems to get anxious about things. She has an ability to ponder things in her heart and when she speaks she always makes so much sense. I have never met a woman like her. John surely loves her, too. Everybody can see it. He will take good care of her. He will treasure the gift that she is.

Jesus, help us to continue to be a child of Mary's. She is suffering so much. Her grief is so deep. First she lost Joseph, and now you. She is a woman who understands grief and mourning. When I'm with her, I feel like she knows me. I feel like I'm her child. It is so peaceful being with her. I just wish I could help her some way. I'll try to treat her like my mother and honor and love her like you do.

"MY GOD, MY GOD, WHY HAVE YOU FORSAKEN ME?"

Jesus, I recognize those words. That psalm is read in the synagogue by the rabbis. But I know those words, because I say them and remember how it was before I met you. I felt so abandoned and forsaken. Oh, I pretended I was strong and didn't care, but on the inside I felt alone and abandoned. My eyes were filled with darkness. My soul was filled with loneliness. It was horrible. Your words pierce my soul. Are you feeling my sin? Jesus, why do you feel my sin? How can you cry out like that, unless sin has covered you over?

Jesus, I want to run and hide. I hear the echo of your cry in my very soul. The power of it vibrates within me. Sin causes pain. It causes pain to the sinner and pain to those that are sinned against. Sin even gets handed down through the generations. It is ugly! It is hurtful and devastating. Darkness of sin makes us alone and abandoned. Jesus, I am repulsed by sin, but I'm drawn to you. Help me to love the sinner and hate the sin. Help me to remember the ugliness of my sin, and sin no more. Jesus, how can I comfort you?

"I THIRST."

Jesus, how I long to quench your thirst. They offer you common wine, vinegary and bitter. Jesus you deserve the choicest wine, the wine that comes from the first harvest, and the wine that has been pressed from the first pressing. That wine is sweet and tasty, pure and clear. Grapes that produce that kind of wine are grown with care and great attention. The vine dresser prunes his vines to insure a succulent crop. The vines are carefully tended. The root is sturdy, but the vines need to be pruned harshly to bring forth the choicest harvest. It is important that the vine dresser prune the vines at the proper time, too soon is as unproductive as too late.

Jesus, I remember you talked about this to us. You said you were the vine and we were the branches. We are the ones who need to be carefully taken care of. We need to be pruned in the proper season. Jesus, you came to me when I was thirsty. I didn't even know how deep my thirst was, until you quenched it. Many were the times you pruned me. For so many years, all I did was produce wild branches, which had little or no fruit. Jesus, allow me to quench your thirst. Make me into choice wine to offer at the banquet table in your Father's kingdom

"IT IS FINISHED."

I hear the cry of the High Priest when the last Passover lamb is slain in the temple for the Passover Feast. "Kalah", it is finished. That's what it was like when you cast the demons from me. It was finished. I knew that I knew it was over. The darkness was gone, and only the light of your love remained. I shouted for joy, full of energy, full of new life. It was done. It was over. My sins had been forgiven. Now you are the Passover Lamb, silent in your sacrifice. Not crying out. Not running from this terrible cross. With dignity, you dance with all the darkness of sin. You do not hesitate or pull back from the pain and suffering inflicted on you.

Jesus, sometimes it is difficult for me to accept pain and suffering. I don't want to be like the paschal lamb. I want to run or at least cry out, "It's not fair". Speech dares silence to have its way. I need to listen to the silence, which is pregnant with sound that only the spirit hears. It is less than a whisper. It reminds me of your embrace, your forgiveness, and your love. Silence speaks loudly, if one has ears to hear.

"FATHER, INTO YOUR HANDS I COMMEND MY SPIRIT."

Jesus, I remember when you told me about going to the river Jordan where your cousin John was baptizing people. He preached about repentance and forgiveness of sin. You wanted to be baptized and he disagreed with you. He knew it was he who needed baptism from you. But John gave in. And he saw the Spirit of God descending like a dove and coming down on you. Now, by accepting this baptism, you said, "yes" to the Father's plan of salvation. It is all finished. You, the sinless one, accepted the sin of mankind. You became the Passover lamb. You endured the suffering. All that was served to you, you embraced. It is finished. Your work is done. With strength and conviction you place that precious Spirit into the Father's hands. In truth this man is the Son of God. Oh, Jesus, I love you.

Jesus calls to each of you. Hear His Seven Last Words. Accept His Seven Last Words. Allow Him to lead you to new life, Life in Their Spirit.

The Last Seven Words

as heard by

Dismas

In Luke's gospel we read about someone called The Good Thief. The gospel does not tell us this thief's name. Tradition calls him Dismas.

You may call me Dismas. In Greek my name means "sunset" or "death". Isn't that an irony? Here I am, a thief, a robber, a man of no worth in this world, hanging on a cross next to this man, Jesus. I am on His right side. There is another man on His left side. All three of us are suffering death by crucifixion. That man in the middle has an inscription on His cross. It says the King of the Jews. He is different from any man I've ever known.

That man in the middle, that Jesus, has died. Soon I too will die. This is my time of "sunset". Death is fast approaching me. But I'm not afraid. I have hope. I am not the same man I was when I was first hung on this cross. I'll never be the same. This is the best day of my life. Oh, I'm still hanging on this cross, but I have hope. I believe!

All of us need HOPE. I invite you to sit back and close your eyes. Listen to the last words of Jesus as He hangs on the cross. Listen to those words through the ears of Dismas.

Dismas was a thief, someone who stole. His encounter with Jesus gave him riches beyond His wildest expectations. In some way, we are all thieves. We want what we don't have. We want belief. We want hope. We want assurance. We want faith. We forget that all we have to do is ask for it. We don't have to steal. Jesus is willing to give us what we want, what we need. We haven't learned how to be like the "good thief". Dismas has words of wisdom for us. Listen to His understandings.

"FATHER, FORGIVE THEM. THEY KNOW NOT WHAT THEY DO."

I had been nailed to my cross before Jesus was nailed to His cross. He impressed me as strong and in control of himself. He never uttered a word when they stretched Him out and drove the nails into Him. The pain is unbearable, but He uttered not a word. He was a sight to behold. He had been scourged repeatedly. His flesh was torn and bleeding. He had this crown of thorns on His head that caused more bleeding. The crowd was jeering. In the midst of this pain and commotion, I saw Jesus pull himself up on the cross. These words issued from His mouth, "Father forgive them. They know not what they do." How could this man think about forgiveness, much less go to the effort to speak these words? He chose to forgive them. What kind of man does this? I'd never seen such patience, such goodness, such mercy. Who was this man? Why would He choose to forgive?

Lord, at times I am part of that jeering crowd refusing to believe that forgiveness is possible. In my pain, forgiveness rarely enters my mind. When I hurt, my pain consumes me. Compassion and mercy elude me. Jesus, I need forgiveness also. Help me to pray for my enemies.

"THIS DAY YOU SHALL BE WITH ME IN PARADISE."

Jesus said those words. He said them to me! Can you imagine my joy and excitement? I would like to tell you how this all happened. The thief that was hanging on His left side said to Jesus, "Are you not the Messiah? Then save yourself and us." I was so ashamed. I know who I am, a sinner. How can that man say such things? He and I are criminals. We are being punished for our crimes, our many sins. That man, Jesus, is NOT a criminal. I know LOVE when I see it. He is the Messiah, but His kingdom is not of this world. He is merciful. I was bold enough to say to Jesus, "Remember me when you come into your kingdom." Looking at me He said, "Amen, I say to you, today you will be with me in Paradise." My heart is full of joy. I know that I know I will be in Paradise with Him today. When you know that your life is full of everything except love and you acknowledge Jesus as your source of love and mercy, He will bring you into paradise with Him TODAY. I recommend that you ask Him to take you into His kingdom. Accept this most wonderful gift. I did.

"WOMAN, BEHOLD YOUR SON. SON, BEHOLD YOUR MOTHER."

There was this woman standing at the foot of the cross before Jesus, silently weeping. She only looked at Jesus. I figured it was His mother. My mother wasn't here with me. Of course, I had long ago given up on my family and they had given up on me. Again, with great effort Jesus pulled himself up on the cross and spoke. He called her Woman. How strange. He said that the man standing near her was her son now. He told the man standing with her to behold her as his mother. Why would a dying man give his mother to another man? There must be something special about her.

Then it happened. She looked over at me. I had never seen such compassion and love except in her Son's eyes. In an instant, I knew that I was loved by her. I was her son. She accepted me just as Jesus had. I want to be in that family. It is truly a family of love and acceptance, a family of mercy. Wouldn't you want to be in that family? Say "yes" to Jesus and His mother.

"MY GOD, MY GOD, WHY HAVE YOU ABANDONED ME?"

Jesus was calling out to God. When He first spoke, He asked His Father to forgive them. Is God His Father? How else could He offer me Paradise today? All this scourging, crucifixion and pain must have cost Him plenty. I know about abandonment. I am the one who abandoned everyone in my life who loved me. It is a choice I made to shut everyone out. The deeper I went into my sinful life making choices to not love, not forgive, not choose to be open and honest and forgiving of everyone in my life, the deeper I felt abandoned. I was all alone because of my own choosing. I didn't know how to get out of my choices.

Then He looked at me with His eyes of love and mercy and I knew the way out. He was my way, my truth and my life. I wanted to follow Him. He will lead me to Paradise, TODAY. Do you feel abandoned, alone, unwanted even by yourself? I tell you Jesus understands and He offers you a new choice.

"I THIRST."

When you are crucified, your lungs thirst for air. When you lose as much blood as Jesus had, your body thirsts for liquids. When you love like Jesus loves, you thirst for everyone to receive that love and forgiveness you offer. That is how I feel about the man on the other side of Jesus. I want him to experience what I am experiencing. I thirst for Him to know LOVE. I thirst for Him to know Jesus.

Jesus called out that He thirst and those soldiers thought they could satisfy Him with that nasty sour wine they offered Him. Jesus accepted their offer. He took what little they could offer. They didn't know what He was saying. Isn't it strange that I know this? Since I said "Yes" to Jesus, it seems like my mind is being renewed. I think differently. I don't know how I know, but I know that Jesus thirsts to love you and me. And I also know He thirsts to be loved by you and me. Jesus, I wish I had more days to quench your thirst. Oh, but I will. I will be in Paradise with you today.

"IT IS FINISHED."

Shortly after Jesus took the wine offered to Him, He said, "It is finished." I must admit, I couldn't help but wonder what IT was. There was a certain sense of satisfaction in His voice. I think it was the type of satisfaction that comes when you have accomplished what you set out to do. I have never experienced that very often. I always seemed to be sidetracked. My life didn't have much of a focus. In fact, I have to admit I wandered from one unfulfilling thing to another. Nothing seemed to satisfy me. Oh, I had plenty of excitement in my life, but it never seemed to last very long. I seemed to always be searching for something, but I never knew what I was searching for.

I wish I would have met this man Jesus before all of this. I am sure He would have helped me see what I couldn't seem to see. But I did get to meet Him, and He told me that today I will be in Paradise with Him. I have hope. He promised me more than I could have ever dreamt of while I was doing my own thing. I know He is a King. I'll gladly be with Him in Paradise. He has changed me and I have hope!!! It is finished.

"FATHER, INTO YOUR HANDS, I COMMEND MY SPIRIT."

I told you, I felt like there was a certain sense of satisfaction in His voice when He said, "It is finished." Shortly after saying, "It is finished", He said in a strong loud voice, "Into your hands I commend my spirit." He bowed His head, just like you do when you come into the presence of someone important, someone you have the highest respect for. Crucifixion is a painful death. You die by inches as the air traps in your lungs. You desire to breath, but you can't breathe out your breath. Ever so slowly you suffocate in your own breath. Despite all that He had suffered, His voice was strong and loud. His voice seemed to say, "you may have done horrible things to my body, you have mocked me and jeered at me, and you have done all that you could to destroy me; but I am telling you that it is of my own free will that I am laying down my life." His voice seems to say, "I am choosing to lay down my life. You can't take my life from me."

"Into your hands, I commend my spirit", and He breathed His last breath. The sun had begun to darken as He was nailed to the cross. It should have been daylight, but now it was dark as night. The earth shook. Jesus had died.

Shortly after Jesus died, Pilate gave the order that the men's legs could be broken to speed up the death process as the solemn Sabbath day was fast approaching. Since Jesus was already dead they didn't break His legs. The legs of the other thief and Dismas' legs were broken and death would have occurred shortly afterwards as the air trapped in their lungs.

The good thief on the cross understood that the kingdom of the King next to him was not of this world. He wanted into that Kingdom. He did not rely on His own merits, or good works. He counted only on the mercy of Jesus. He said, "Remember me." The good thief had recognized His sins, renounced His past, accepted His cross in the present moment and desired only the reward promised by Jesus. Today He lives in Paradise with Jesus. Where will you live for all eternity?

The Last Seven Words

as heard by

Mother of Zebedee's Sons

We are gathered here today because the Passion of Jesus has drawn us. We humans have a natural curiosity when a person dies. We want to hear what their last words were before they died. Fortunately for us, the Bible has recorded these last words of Jesus. Today, I would invite you to imagine the scene at the crucifixion. Hear these words through the filter of the mother of the sons' of Zebedee.

I was there when they crucified Jesus. I was standing with Mary and the other women. It might seem strange to your ears to hear that I had followed Him from Galilee to attend to His needs. Jesus has a way of calling each of us and we find ourselves doing things we never dreamt of doing.

My sons are John and James, disciples of Jesus. My husband is Zebedee. He is a fisherman in Galilee. My boys were fishermen too, that is before Jesus called them. Like I said, Jesus has a way of calling us and we find ourselves doing things we never dreamt of doing. I am a good Jewish mother. I always wanted the best for "my boys". That is only natural; every mother wants the best for their children. I have to tell you, I was disturbed and angry when my boys left to follow this Jesus. My husband had worked hard to build up our fishing business. We had a good reputation and a fine business. Of course, we expected our boys to carry on the business. What mother wouldn't be upset to have her boys leave the family dream?

Much has happened to me in the three years since Jesus called my sons. I didn't follow Him immediately like my sons did. Discipleship is costly, it demands leaving family and financial security. It took me some time to trust and believe Him. Actually, it was only when I heard that Jesus was heading down from Galilee to Jerusalem that I decided to go along with my sons and follow Jesus. I went with His mother and some other women.

I have to tell you what I did just before we got to Jericho, that place where the walls had come tumbling down. I came up to Jesus, out of respect for what I had been hearing about the kingdom, to ask a favor. I wanted His promise that my sons would sit one at His left and one at His right in this kingdom. He quickly told me that I didn't know what I was asking. Could I drink of the cup He was going to drink? We were quick to say we could. Imagine our surprise when Jesus explained three important facts about the kingdom to us; first of all, a place in the kingdom demands suffering, secondly, it is NOT Jesus' job to determine status in the coming kingdom, and thirdly, leadership in Jesus' kingdom means service.

We went into Jericho and met those two blind men. Jesus asked them, "What do you want from me?" They answered, "Lord, open our eyes." I prayed that with them. "Open my eyes Lord that I truly can comprehend, believe and follow the ways of your kingdom."

"FATHER, FORGIVE THEM. THEY KNOW NOT WHAT THEY DO."

Forgive them. This man Jesus is so strange. He forgives, even when we don't know what we are doing. Just like me. I just wanted the best for my boys. I didn't understand about Kingdom living. I have servants. They do what I tell them to do. They are obedient to what I say. Jesus told me that leadership in the kingdom meant being a Servant. I'm not sure that I will be able to be a servant. I am used to being in control. Living like Jesus in the kingdom will mean I will have to let others have control. That will be difficult. Maybe I won't be able to drink of the cup of forgiveness that Jesus offers me.

Dear Jesus, see my fears. I am afraid to offer forgiveness to another, I want to be right. I want to be in control. I want to be in a position of power and prestige. My heart needs changing. Forgive me. Forgive me for the times of my blindness. Forgive me for seeking MY honor, MY glory. Only now can I begin to see that what I thought was so right, is really contrary to Kingdom living. Jesus forgive me, I didn't know what I was doing.

"THIS DAY YOU WILL BE WITH ME IN PARADISE."

"OH, Yahweh, have mercy. What is He saying?" Jesus heard the taunts of the people. He heard the thief hanging next to Him say, "So you're the Messiah, are you? Prove it by saving yourself—and us, too, while you're at it." I saw Him turn His head and look with compassion at that thief. He uttered not a word. On His other side was another thief. This thief rebuked his comrade in crime, "Don't you even fear God when you're dying? We deserve to die for the evil we have done, but this man hasn't done anything wrong." Then he said, "Jesus, remember me when you come into your Kingdom." Jesus said, "Today, you will be with me in Paradise." Can you really believe that? Adam and Eve caused us to be banished from Paradise. Jesus is saying that the Kingdom is in Paradise

.Jesus, my whole belief system has to change. When you banished Adam and Eve from the Garden, from Paradise, no one ever entered in again. Jesus, you told the thief that knew his wrong way of living, that Paradise could be his today. Only the Messiah, the Holy One of God, has the right to open the gates of Paradise. Jesus, I believe, that I too can enter into Paradise with you today. Jesus, allow your Kingdom to come in me. Allow me to do your will here on earth as it is done in Paradise.

"WOMAN, BEHOLD YOUR SON. SON, BEHOLD YOUR MOTHER."

Remember, I told you I had been traveling down from Galilee with Mary, Jesus' mother, and some other women. It gave me an opportunity to watch her and her son together. I know my boys love me. But there is something so special about their relationship. They truly love one another. Jesus is suffering on that cross, but so is His mother. I just want to take her in my arms and console her. She is suffering so greatly. Jesus said a place in the kingdom demands suffering. I wonder if He realized how much she would suffer with Him. Oh, the look that passes between them as He utters those words. My heart hurts as I see their pain.

Dear Jesus, my love pales when I witness the love between your mother and you. You are so willing to suffer and she is so willing to suffer with you. Jesus, you know me. I run from suffering. It hurts. It is painful. It is not pretty. Remember, I wanted the best for my boys. I didn't want them to suffer. Isn't there any other way for the kingdom to come, except through suffering? Help me to know that whenever suffering comes my way, you and your mother will be with me as I go through it. Let your Kingdom come.

"MY GOD, MY GOD, WHY HAVE YOU FORSAKEN ME?"

Oh Jesus, you feel abandoned, deserted. That is just how I feel when I am truly suffering. I feel so unloved, so forsaken. I know the Psalm that Jesus quotes. It is one of my favorites. It is a Psalm of Hope. This Psalm is describing the scene before my eyes. Jesus' strength is being drained away. His bones are out of joint. His hands and feet are pierced. They have divided His clothes with a toss of the dice. It describes a great suffering amidst a mocking, sneering crowd. O God, don't stay away. O God, my Strength, hurry to my aid.

Yahweh, Jesus calls to you. Just like the Israelites of old. The Psalm reminds me that with all of Israel I sing His praises. The Psalm goes on to say that God has not despised my cries of deep despair, He has not turned and walked away. When I cried to Him, He heard and came. Jesus called God His Father. Today He calls to the God of Israel, to the Great I AM. He too has put His trust in the Great I AM. Jesus, help me to cling to that kind of trust when I am in suffering. Help me to remember, God hears when I call to Him in my darkest hours, in my times of suffering.

"I THIRST."

In that same Psalm, it describes someone whose throat is dried up like baked clay. Jesus thirsts. He who promised to be the source of Living Water thirsts. Common wine, like vinegar, is offered to Him. My boys have told me that they often heard Him say, His food and drink was to do the will of His Father. Can this truly be the will of His Father? If God is His Father, shouldn't He be given a place of honor? Jesus told me that giving a place of honor wasn't His to give. Surely His Father sees what is happening to His son.

Jesus, it feels so much better to be honored and hold a position of prestige and power. Doing the will of the Father led you to the cross. You accepted wine of the common people for your thirst. How I rebel when I am common, when I am not noticed, when I am not treated with respect and honor. Jesus, I need your humility. I need to grow in my obedience to the Father's will for me.

"IT IS FINISHED."

He seems to know it is over. He has suffered much. It is difficult to speak when you are being crucified, yet each of His words seemed well chosen. I've heard His words and I know I will think about them often. I truly thought I could drink of the cup He was to drink . What a foolish woman I am. He is like a sheep led to slaughter, docile and obedient, yet fully alive to each precious moment. He seems to know that what He had to do is finished. There was a confidence, almost a joy, when He said those words.

Each day I have is a gift from you. I truly desire to drink of the cup you drank, but I see my limitations. I see all those parts of me that still want to run from conflict, chaos, and confrontation. I want to be obedient to the Father's will; but fear, sloth, and immaturity keep me from saying "Yes". Please, dear Jesus, help me to grow in wisdom, age and grace before your Father.

"FATHER, INTO YOUR HANDS I COMMEND MY SPIRIT."

My boys told me a story about Jesus calling himself the Good Shepherd. He told them, "No one can kill me without my consent—I lay down my life voluntarily. For I have the right and power to lay it down when I want to and also the right and power to take it again. For the Father has given me this right." As I said before, there was a confidence in His voice when He said, "It is finished." Did you just hear Him? I heard a shout of victory. He was willingly laying down His life. No one could be mistaken about it. He shouted triumphantly and trustingly to His Father.

That is what it is like when you drink of the cup Jesus offers you with a willing spirit and understanding heart. When I said I wanted to drink of the cup, Jesus was quick to tell me that I really didn't understand what I was asking. I understand more clearly now that drinking of the cup means a willingness to lay down my life for my brothers and sisters. That doesn't bring a guarantee of status or honor. Drinking of Jesus' cup means being willing to be a suffering servant, being willing to be obedient to the Father's will for me this day with this person in these circumstances. Greater love has no man or woman than to lay down their life for another.

The Last Seven Words

as heard by

The Beloved Disciple

In John's gospel, we read of those standing at the foot of the cross. There is one there who is called the disciple Jesus loved. Many believe this was John. A BELOVED DISCIPLE listening to the words of Jesus as He hung on the cross would have heard these words differently than the average person listening to these words.

Do you know you are His Beloved? Anyone who lets Jesus love him can be the Beloved Disciple. You, me, and anyone who comes to know the love of Jesus is the Beloved Disciple. Jesus spoke His Seven Last Words for us, His Beloved Ones!

"Have you ever wondered what I would have said to you if you had been at my side as Peter, John, Mary, Martha, and the rest? Do you feel that they were especially favored to have lived when they did, because they saw me, heard me, and touched me? Yes, they were favored. But so are you. It is better for you to live now than at any other time in human history. Do you not realize that this is my hour just as much as it was twenty centuries ago? I see you as clearly as I saw them. I love you as I loved them. I speak to you! You are my Beloved Disciple. Listen to My words."

Jesus, I heard you. I know I am your Beloved. At least, I know that in my head. Sometimes it is difficult to believe that in my heart. When suffering comes, when my prayers aren't answered in a way I expect them to be answered, and when life is difficult and lonely, I truly have a difficult time believing that I really am your Beloved.

Once, I read a book by a famous contemporary author, Henri Nouwen. He said that, "self-rejection is the greatest enemy of the spiritual life because self rejection contradicts the sacred voice that calls us the Beloved.

Jesus, here and now, I choose to believe you call me your Beloved

"FATHER, FORGIVE THEM. THEY KNOW NOT WHAT THEY DO."

Isn't that a strange statement? All through the gospels we see Jesus forgiving people. In fact, that is what infuriated the Pharisees about Jesus. Who did He think He was to forgive sin? That is God's role.

Remember Jesus is the God-Man. It seems as if He spoke this first word as Son of Man, not as Son of God. He does not cling to His divinity but, rather, asks His Father to forgive them. Who is "them?" The Romans, the high priest, the ones pounding the nails, His disciples who have deserted Him; they all need forgiveness. But so do we, and so did our ancestors before us, and those

who will come after us. We have all fallen short of the mark. Jesus is asking His Father to forgive them through Himself. He is offering to be our scapegoat. He is offering to die for our sins. Truly, we are one of "them".
Jesus you were born without sin. During your lifetime, you did not sin. Yours was a life of loving. I know myself. I am a sinner. How can I possibly call myself your Beloved, when I know the darkness of my own sin? Jesus, am I truly your Beloved, despite the darkness of my sin?

"THIS DAY YOU SHALL BE WITH ME IN PARADISE."

He hung between two thieves, like a common criminal. Those thieves made fun of Him just as the crowd was taunting Him. Jesus spoke not a word. His silence must have spoken to the one thief's heart. Or was it the previous word Jesus had spoken when He asked the Father to forgive them that touched the thief's heart? Whatever grace moves him, he asks Jesus to remember him when He comes into His reign. Jesus tells him that this day you will be with me in paradise. Jesus knows He controls the gates to paradise.

What words of Jesus move your heart? Jesus says He is the way, the truth and the life, and no one comes to the Father, but through Him. He has the ability to open the gates of paradise to a convicted thief and He has the ability to open those gates for you. Faith in God's grace opened the door and invited the thief in. Faith opens those same doors for you.

Jesus, which of your words have I allowed into my heart? Jesus, I am sorry for not reading my bible more often. You want to speak to me, but I don't take time to listen. During this Lent, I tried to spend time with you in the Blessed Sacrament. I found out how noisy my interior life is, but I tried to allow the silence to speak to my heart. I am convinced that you want to love me. I am convinced that you want me in paradise with you. But am I convinced you call me your Beloved?

"WOMAN, BEHOLD YOUR SON. SON, BEHOLD YOUR MOTHER."

Jesus calls her Woman, just as He did at Cana. He knows she is the new Eve. By identifying His mother as "Woman" He is telling us He is the offspring of the Woman who will crush Satan's head. She is the Woman who so clearly was obedient to the Father's will. Jesus wants her to know that her role is expanded. As once she carried Jesus in Her womb, she now is given to the Beloved Disciple. Jesus knows the jewel His mother is and He offers her to the Beloved Disciple. To be chosen to receive Jesus' mother as our mother is such an act of love. The Beloved Disciple accepts this most wondrous gift.

Jesus knows we need a relationship with Mary. He knows her heart. He is not fearful that she will take any of His glory. Jesus knows His mother will always lead us to her Son. Mary said yes to the role of "woman" when she said her fiat. She knew the Father looked at her lowliness. But she also knew that all ages to come would call her blessed.

If the Beloved Disciple stands for every disciple, then he stands for each of us. Beloved Disciples welcome the gift of Mary, as their Mother. Beloved Disciples are not afraid to call her Mother. As the sorrowful Mother at the foot of the cross, Mary remains the suffering Mother who prays not to lose the children Jesus gave her on Calvary. Mary is the Mother of the Beloved Disciple and us.

"MY GOD, MY GOD, WHY HAVE YOU FORSAKEN ME?"

It is noon and darkness is coming over the whole land. Jesus is silent. The witnesses to the crucifixion stand watching, but even more they are listening to the labored breathing of Jesus. Jesus remains silent. Nearly three hours pass when the silence is broken by a loud cry, a thundering cry. Jesus is no longer calling His Father. He is calling God. Jesus senses that our sins have covered Him. Christians know when we sin; our sin separates us from God. Jesus feels the horrible agony of being separated from His God. His cry is a desperate cry of separation. He believes God has forsaken Him. He believes He is the scapegoat. All the sinful faults and transgressions are put on Him. But Jesus believes His being forsaken by God means that we the Beloved Disciples are acceptable to God.

In Hebrews 13:5&6 we read, "I will never desert you, nor will I forsake you." Thus, we may say with confidence, "The Lord is my helper, I will not be afraid." Did you really hear that? God will NEVER forsake you. Romans 8:1 tells us, "There is no condemnation now for those who are in Christ Jesus." Beloved Disciples know in their hearts that Jesus' death on the cross paid the price in full for all of their sins. Beloved Disciples do not have to worry about being forsaken.

"I THIRST."

There are many prophecies about Jesus in the Old Testament. Psalm 69:21 says, "In my thirst they gave me vinegar to drink. Just as predicted, when Jesus says "I thirst" they offer Him vinegar to drink. Jesus certainly would be experiencing physical thirst after all He has been through. He asks for comfort and He gets the drink of the poor man, common vinegary wine served on a hyssop branch. Jesus understands what it is to be human. Often we cry out for help and receive only the smallest compassion from our brothers and sisters. Our greatest thirst is to know God.

A Beloved Disciple continues to thirst for more of God's love. Beloved Disciples are not fearful of that thirst. They have come to know that despite how difficult the circumstances of their lives, they have a savior who has gone before them. Our savior, Jesus Christ, was not afraid to admit His human needs. He was thirsty. Beloved Disciples are human beings and, too, thirst for all Jesus thirsts for. Beloved Disciples know that the Holy Spirit living within them is a well that never runs dry. The Holy Spirit forever wants us to know God better and better.

"IT IS FINISHED."

Jesus said everything He was called to do as the Messiah is finished. Every prophecy spoken in the Old Testament about the Messiah is fulfilled. In John 4:34, we read these words of Jesus, "Doing the will of Him who sent me and bringing His work to completion is my food." Jesus completed this task; His work is finished. Nothing more is needed. Our debt has been paid in full.

Jesus can say, "It is finished." It is a different story for you and me. We are Beloved Disciples, but we have such a long history of starting things and not finishing them. We have good intentions. But when pain, suffering or frustration overcomes us, we grow fearful, anxious and short-sighted. We seem to lack the grit to go the last mile. St. Paul knew he was a Beloved Disciple. He gives us advice in His letter to the Hebrews. Hebrews 12:2 says, "Let us keep our eyes fixed on Jesus, who inspires and perfects our faith. For the sake of the joy which lay before Him He endured the cross heedless of its shame."

"FATHER, INTO YOUR HANDS, I COMMEND MY SPIRIT."

Phil 2:6-8 says, "Though He was in the form of God, He did not deem equality with God something to be grasped at. Rather, He emptied himself and took the form of a slave, being born in the likeness of men. He was known to be of HUMAN estate, and it was thus that He humbled himself, obediently accepting even death, death on a cross." Jesus came a long way from His agony in the garden. Obedience to His Father was always His purpose. His temptations were always to use His divine powers to handle human situations. Jesus knows what it is to be a human being. Jesus lived His life fully. He now can say to His Father once more, "my life and my death are in your hands." It is into your loving hands, Father, that I commend my spirit. I deliver with confidence my spirit into your hands, Father.

1Cor15:55-58 says, "Death is swallowed up in victory. O Death, where is your victory? O death, where is your sting? The sting of death is sin, and sin gets its power from the law. But thanks be to God who has given us the victory through our Lord Jesus Christ."

Just as I died, so shall you.
Just as I suffered, so shall you.
Just as I was appointed to a task, so are you.
Just as I bore fruit, so shall you.

I have appointed you a task, to bear fruit, to be my witness. For this reason, you live at this time, in this nation, in this community, under these particular circumstances. I have called you my Beloved. Your love is a love that rests in the heart of God. Understand that no amount of suffering, not even death itself could have redeemed you. Love redeemed you, the love I have for my Father. The love I have for you. You are my Beloved.

The Last Seven Words

as heard by

John, Son of Thunder

Jesus spoke seven times from the cross, or His Seven Last Words. These words have been handed down over the centuries for our remembrance. Today, I invite you to stop awhile and reflect on these words. Allow the Holy Spirit to take you deeper into the meaning of these words of Jesus. Every word spoken by Jesus is life for the listener.

I have a story to tell you, on this day that you remember the death of Jesus. I was there. I watched it all. I'll never forget that day. My name is John. I am the son of Zebedee. I am a fisherman. My brother's name is James. We lived by the Sea of Galilee. One day while we were fishing, Jesus came by. He called to us. I heard His call and I obeyed His invitation. Immediately I abandoned my boat and my father and followed Him. I never dreamt it would lead to This day.

Jesus is like no other man I've ever met. Yet He is just like you and me. He came from Nazareth, yet often He talked about His heavenly home with His Father. He seemed to know me when we met, though I had never met Him before. He gave my brother and me a strange name. He called us **"sons of thunder"**. We thought about that name many times.

My life has never been the same since He called me. I have been with Him over three years now. I am pleased to tell you, I am one of His twelve companions. Living with Him has been one adventure after another. Over the years we've been together, He taught me many things. I surely had much to learn. He would send us out to preach the good news. When we did, miracles followed. He gave us authority to expel demons and heal the sick. Jesus is quite a man. I could tell you about when He took Peter, James and me up on Mt. Tabor. I couldn't speak for all that happened up there. He was transfigured and I heard a voice like **thunder**.

Last night was Passover. We surely had a celebration. He washed my feet. He told us He was the bread of life and gave us the bread to eat. Jesus said He'd give us His blood for drink, and He did. He told us not to let our hearts be troubled. He promises to send the Holy Spirit when He comes into His glory. Once my mother came to Him wanting for us to be at His right hand in that kingdom. He told her she didn't know what she was asking for, that we'd have to drink from the cup He was to drink of. I think this is the cup He was talking about then. He seemed to know this was going to happen to Him. He told us about it. Sometimes it is difficult to believe all He tells you. Fear wants to crowd out His words.

"FATHER, FORGIVE THEM. THEY KNOW NOT WHAT THEY DO."

Forgive them. Isn't that just like Him? He is always ready to forgive. He always loves His enemies. Look at what He has suffered already. The shame, humiliation, scourging, crowning with thorns, carrying His cross through town like a common criminal, and now being nailed to that cross. He is not a criminal. He is an innocent victim. Can't you see that? Why are your eyes so blinded? His Father was always on His mind. And His Father's kingdom. I remember Mary told me that when He was twelve He had stayed on in Jerusalem during the Passover. When she and Joseph finally found Him in the temple, all He could say was, "Don't you know that I must be about my Father's business". He cries to the Father to forgive them. Is that me too, Jesus? I know that many times, I am unaware of being about the Father's business. Sometimes I don't even know where the Father's kingdom is in a situation.

Dear Jesus, in my own way I have failed you. I hope that as you call to the Father, you are remembering me too. I know that you love me, but sometime I doubt your love. Sometime I doubt that the Father and you will forgive me. That is not what you taught. You told me again and again how much the Father loves me. He wants me to spend eternity in His kingdom.

"THIS DAY YOU WILL BE WITH ME IN PARADISE."

When our brother Adam sinned, the Lord God banished him from the Garden of Eden. Paradise, that beautiful Garden of God. That place that eye has not seen, nor ear heard, nor has it entered into the hearts of man what God has prepared for those who love Him. There are two thieves hanging on either side of Jesus. One taunts Him. The other asks to be remembered when Jesus comes into the kingdom. Jesus has the authority to bring us into paradise. His Father gave Him that authority. I know it is His authority, as demons flee at His name. Sickness goes in His name. It is the name of Jesus and His authority that will bring me into the kingdom.

Dear Jesus, hear my cry. Just like that thief upon the cross, I cry out to you, "Remember me in the Kingdom." I trust in you to bring me into Paradise. I know that like Adam I deserve to be banished from your garden, but I choose to have a heart like the "good thief". I cry out to you for mercy and forgiveness. Jesus, This Day, I accept your promise that I am in paradise with you.

"WOMAN, BEHOLD YOUR SON. SON, BEHOLD YOUR MOTHER."

To know Jesus is to know His mother. What a woman she is! I wish you could see them together. Their love and respect for each other radiates from them. He speaks, she listens. She speaks, He listens. I told you I never met a man like

Jesus, well, I never met a woman like Mary. She has this knack for pondering. She takes in all that He says, and then is able to respond completely and fully. Jesus your mother is filled with sorrow as she stands here at the foot of the cross. How honored I am that you give her to me.
    Jesus, my hearts leaps with joy. My mind swirls trying to comprehend all that is happening. I love your mother. I want to take care of her, but I am so aware it will be her that cares for me. Jesus what a precious gift you give to me. Jesus, that you trust me to your mother. You must love me to give me your treasure. I look at her and she has momentarily taken her eyes off of you. She looks with love and compassion at her child.

"MY GOD, MY GOD, WHY HAVE YOU FORSAKEN ME?"

    Jesus, I recognize those words. They are the words of the Psalms. "Oh God, why have you left me? Why are you so far from me? I can no longer feel you near. I know you are holy and everywhere present, but I cannot find you. I risked all to follow what I thought was your will for me. Even my friends fail to support me. I believed you were with me from the very beginning of my life, but God, I need you now. I am in trouble. I can't find you or feel you near me. I feel weak. God help me." His words pierce my soul.
    Father, hear the cry of your child in anguish. Darkness and despairing feelings try to overwhelm me. But you, O Father, are not far from me. You know both my feelings and my failings, yet you love me and accept me. You will rescue my soul. You will rescue me out of my loneliness. I dedicate myself anew to you. I will serve you whatever the cost or the consequence. Regardless of my feelings of weakness and insecurity, I will praise your name and proclaim your love. You hear my cries and feel my pain and are ever ready to be there with me.

"I THIRST."

    Jesus thirsts. He has lost much blood and the hour grows late. He asks for a drink. He is in need, as one hoping to receive. Yet He is rich, as one about to satisfy the thirst of others. He spoke so often of living waters flowing from Him. The Samaritan Woman knew what He was talking about and through her the whole town came to believe in those life-giving waters. They offer Him common wine, vinegary and bitter. He drinks it. They have no idea what it is that He thirsts for. Their drink would never satisfy Him.
    Jesus is thirsty. I can hear Him say, "Give souls to me. Give me souls that they may experience how good, how wonderful it is to live in my Father's love. See how much I love them; how much I want to be near them always." He was promising the Holy Spirit in satisfying abundance. "Whoever drinks the water I

shall give will never be thirsty again." He was speaking of the Spirit who would be received by those who believed in Him. Jesus, I know I am your Beloved Disciple. I know that you love me. I know your love for me has taken you to this cross. Dear Jesus, help me to quench your thirst.

"IT IS FINISHED."

It is finished. Your message, your task, why you came has been completed. It is finished. When the high priest has slaughtered the last Passover Lamb He cries out, "It is finished". What more is there to say? What more is there to do? You were that silent obedient lamb led to a slaughter you didn't deserve. You are the acceptable sacrifice. For all these days that I have been with you, you have been showing me this day. Over and over in veiled and outspoken words, you have told me of this day. How slow I am to comprehend. My heart believed, but my mind had to be enlightened.

Dear Jesus, it is finished. Silence descends upon me. There is no further sound. It is finished. It is over. Days of quiet on the Sea of Galilee are over. Walking the dusty roads with you is over. Hearing your voice as you call my name is over. Listening to your voice as you talked about the kingdom is over. Jesus, my hearts aches. There is such sadness. All is quiet.

"FATHER, INTO YOUR HANDS I COMMEND MY SPIRIT."

Thunder! His voice was as strong as **thunder**! "Father, into your hands I commend my spirit." It didn't matter to Him that all would not believe and understand what He had just done for us. It was finished and He knew that He knew it was over. He had been the obedient son. He had done the Father's will. He could shout triumphantly to His Father, "Daddy into your hands I commend my spirit. Daddy into your hands I can deliver with confidence my spirit". He knew His father was very fond of Him.

Jesus, you gave James and me the name of "sons of thunder". I've always wondered why you called us that. Now I know so clearly. I am your Beloved. The Father and you love me. There is nothing that can separate me from your love. Your love is everlasting.

I remember when we began this journey to Jerusalem. We had to pass through a Samaritan town. The Samaritans would not welcome you. I was angry. I remembered I asked, "Lord, would you not have us call down fire from heaven to destroy them?" You turned toward me and reprimanded me. Your look and your words pierced my heart. Now I understand. I will never call down fire from heaven to destroy. I will spend the rest of my life calling out, as **thunder**, the words of our Father, "This is my Beloved Son, hear Him."

The Last Seven Words

as heard by

Nicodemus

The Passion of Jesus is a topic in the minds and hearts of many today. We have had an opportunity to view the crucifixion on the big screen. Today, I would invite you to listen to the Words that Jesus spoke. The Gospels tell us of Seven Words that Jesus spoke from the cross. I would invite you to pray for the grace to hear the words that Jesus speaks. Words are capable of moving the hearts of people, even today, two thousand years later.

My name is Nicodemus. I am a Pharisee, a member of the Sanhedrin. Words have always caused me to ponder. Jesus spoke words that caught people by surprise. He was so confident when He spoke. His words had power to reach the coldest of hearts. My heart was cold at one time. I came to Him in the night, in darkness, my own darkness. I knew Jesus was a teacher, and I knew the signs and wonders He had performed. No one could have done these things if God wasn't with Him. Do you know what He said to me? "I solemnly assure you, unless you are born again, you can never enter into the Kingdom of God." That made me angry in my fear. "How can a man be born again once he is old? Can one return to His mother's womb and be born over again?"

Jesus replied, "I solemnly assure you, unless one is born of water and the Spirit, he cannot enter the Kingdom of God. Men can only reproduce human life, but the Holy Spirit gives new life from heaven"

I was indignant, how can such a thing happen? Like I said His words are powerful, and His response went deep into my heart. Jesus also said to me, "You hold the office of teacher of Israel and still you do not understand these matters? I solemnly assure you, we are talking about what we know, we are testifying to what we have seen, but you do not accept our testimony. The Son of Man must be lifted up, that all who believe in Him may have eternal life. God loved the world so much that He gave His only Son, so that anyone who believes in Him shall not die, but have eternal life. God did not send His Son into the world to condemn the world, but to save it."

"FATHER, FORGIVE THEM. THEY KNOW NOT WHAT THEY DO."

Forgive us!! He is asking the Father to forgive me. I was a coward. I couldn't defend Him. Once, during one of our High Feast Days, Jesus was teaching in the temple. Guards were sent to arrest Him, but they came back without Him. All that the guards could say was they never heard anyone like Him. I understood what they were saying. The Pharisees, all of the Sanhedrin, wanted Him arrested I asked if it was legal to convict a man before he is tried. They laughed at me and challenged my knowledge of the scriptures. This man is like no one I have known. He is being crucified, in such pain, and He asks that we be forgiven.

Dear Jesus, so often in our lives we need to hear these words of yours. Forgiving myself is not easy. Forgiveness isn't always something we are willing to offer those who offend us. It is easier to grow angry and seek vengeance of my own choosing. I have never experienced the amount of pain you suffered, yet I am so reluctant to extend forgiveness. My pride stands in the way. Please Jesus take my pride, teach me your ways of forgiveness.

"THIS DAY YOU WILL BE IN PARADISE."

This man Jesus offers paradise to a common thief. He offers him Paradise, the Divine Dwelling Place. I know from the scriptures that God cast man out of the Divine Dwelling Place. God put mighty angels with flaming swords to guard its entrance. Jesus says to this common thief that he can enter Paradise, today. The thief had said, "Jesus, remember me when you come into your kingdom." Do you suppose, I could receive Paradise too?

Jesus, I have read of the sin of my first parents. I know they were shut out of Paradise. God had walked and talked to them in the Garden. Jesus, if you can offer Paradise to a thief who recognizes your sinlessness, I know you can offer that restored relationship to me. I recognize you are without sin. I recognize my many sins. Have mercy on me. This day bring me into Paradise, that Divine Dwelling Place.

"WOMAN, BEHOLD YOUR SON. SON, BEHOLD YOUR MOTHER."

I see this woman standing at the foot of the cross. How can a mother be willing to stand and watch her son being crucified? The agony she must feel! She has to be willing to suffer, just as her son is suffering. I believe that the man with her is one of His followers. I wonder why this Jesus is so concerned about His mother at a time like this. What is so special about her?

Jesus, so many people don't know your mother. They almost seem fearful to acknowledge her. She is the one whose "yes" made your birth possible. She is the one who says, "Do whatever He tells you." She is the one who calls attention to the needs of others. She is the one who always leads us back to you. Jesus, I want a better relationship with your mother. I truly want her to be a mother to me. I want to experience her, just as you experienced her.

"MY GOD, MY GOD, WHY HAVE YOU FORSAKEN ME?"

I know those words. They are the words of my brother, King David. I have heard them many times. They take on new meaning as I gaze on this man, Jesus. He is forsaken. No one can rescue Him. His bones are racked, His hands and feet are pierced, and they are casting lots for His garments. He is surrounded by fearsome enemies. But I know the end of that Psalm. It says," the Lord is King and rules the nations. Both proud and humble together, all who are mortal—born to die—shall worship him. Our children too shall serve Him, for they shall hear from us about the wonders of the Lord, generations yet unborn shall hear of all the miracles He did for us." Could it be? Is this Jesus truly a King?

Jesus, at the hour of your greatest suffering, you remembered the words of your scriptures. It was all there, to the smallest detail. This is the Father's will for you. You have been that "good and faithful servant". Jesus, I too, will suffer in this life. There will be hardships of my own making. There will be times of distress because of others. In all situations Jesus, help me to remember you and call upon you for strength and perseverance. Help me when I feel forsaken, but especially help me to recognize you as my Lord and King.

"I THIRST."

Jesus is thirsting. The sun was high overhead, enough to make anyone thirst. One of the guards offers Jesus a sponge soaked in common wine. He holds it up to Jesus on some hyssop. My mind goes to the Passover that we celebrate each year. We used hyssop dipped in the blood of the lamb to protect us that fateful night. The sponge is held to His mouth, the wine dribbles down His chin and mixes with His shed blood. Oh Yahweh, is He the Lamb to be slain for us all? Is this our King?

Jesus, I thirst for truth. Are you really the Messiah, the long awaited one? I believe you are. I believe you are the Lamb. You were slain for my sins and the sins of all. It is your shed blood, so very precious, that brings me salvation. Jesus never let me partake of your blood without remembering the price you paid that I might drink it new in the Father's Kingdom.

"IT IS FINISHED."

What is finished? How does He know it is finished? He said He came to do His Father's will. All that the Father had asked of Him must be done. His work is completed. What a good feeling it must be, to know at the end of your life you have completed everything. I know when we slaughter the final lamb for Passover, we say, "It is finished." Does He see himself as the Paschal Lamb? Is that why He calls out, "It is finished" with such authority? His words were so carefully chosen, spoken with such conviction.

Jesus, can I say to you, "It is finished."? Can I trust you to take away my addictions? Can I say, "They are finished"? Can I trust you to heal all the wounds in my mind and body? Can I say, "They are healed."? Can I trust you to defeat the evil in my life? Can I say, "Satan, you and your kingdom are finished."? Can I trust you to heal all my relationships? Can I say, "I forgive all who have trespassed against me."? Jesus, help me with my desires to say, "It is finished."

"FATHER, INTO YOUR HANDS I COMMEND MY SPIRIT."

With confidence, He entrusts His Spirit to His Father. He openly told people that God was His Father. How foreign that sounded to our ears. How blatantly arrogant He was to call God His Father. I told you His words are powerful. They have a way of going to the heart of a person. They are words that often the mind cannot understand; only the heart can. My heart understands. God is His Father! He is the Son of God! Oh, my heart fills with such JOY!

Nicodemus came with Joseph of Arimathea to take Jesus' body away for burial. He brought a hundred pounds of myrrh and aloes for the occasion. That is the amount prescribed for the burial of a King. Pilate had written, Jesus the Nazorean the King of the Jews. Nicodemus knew Jesus was His King.

I am like Nicodemus, I come in my darkness seeking God's Truth. My life is a journey. I will meet ridicule for my beliefs along the pathway, just as Nicodemus did. I will search and search for the Truth. I will watch and listen to the words of the Scriptures. One day my heart will overflow with a joy that cannot be taken from me.

The Last Seven Words

as heard by

Joseph of Arimathea

Living in the United States allows us a freedom of speech and a freedom of assembly. So today we can gather together and remember our Savior, Jesus. We do not have to keep our relationship with Jesus a secret. In fact, we are called to evangelize.

You have been walking the way of the cross with this man Jesus, but I wonder if you'd recognize me on this walk. I doubt it! For you see, it was very important to me that my association with Jesus was kept a secret. I am Joseph of Arimathea. I am a distinguished member of the Sanhedrin, the supreme council of my Jewish nation. I am a Sadducee. My views and practices are opposed to those of the Pharisees. Unlike my Pharisee brothers, I don't believe the existence of angels and the resurrection of the dead. Like every good Jew, I had been looking expectantly for the reign of God. Then I met Jesus. I was His disciple, although a secret one. I had too much to risk if my relationship was out in the open. After all, one must maintain their reputation and their position.

It was only after His death that I could find the courage in myself to go boldly to Pilate and ask permission to remove Jesus' body from the cross. Because of my wealth, I'd already had a tomb prepared for my own burial. I choose to lay Jesus' body in my tomb. It was only a short distance from where he was crucified. My friend Nicodemus, also a member of the Sanhedrin, came with me. He brought a hundred pounds of spices to help with the burial.

Carefully, we took the body of Jesus off the cross, and laid Him in the waiting arms of His mother, Mary. When I saw her receive the broken body of her son, then the words I heard Him speak from the cross became much clearer. Why, I can hear them again in my spirit.

"FATHER, FORGIVE THEM. THEY KNOW NOT WHAT THEY DO."

Jesus was speaking to me. My silence, my secrecy, was offensive. I had never met a man like Jesus. He won my heart after just a few encounters. There was something different about this man. The longer I listened to what he said, the clearer some things became. Oh, I don't mean that everything was understandable. He had some hard sayings. He challenged me with His beliefs. When you are a member of the Sanhedrin, you are always listening for the truth in the light of the law. He challenged my concept of "An eye for an eye, a tooth for a tooth". Forgiveness is not an easy saying. Sometimes one can look intently and not see truth, listen carefully and not hear truth. One needs to repent and be forgiven for the hardness of one's heart.

Jesus, please take the hardness of my heart and give me the grace to forgive as you do.

"THIS DAY YOU WILL BE WITH ME IN PARADISE."

Why when I heard those words, I shuddered. Jesus told the repentant thief that he and the thief would be in the same place together, Paradise, and on this day. I told you some of His sayings are difficult to understand. So often they stretched me to a breaking point. The thief repents, forgiveness occurs, and he is on His way to paradise with Jesus. My mind could scarcely take it in. Paradise is a place for the righteous and the victorious. He was a common thief. He said so. He told the other thief who was taunting Jesus, "We deserve this. We are only paying the price for what we've done, but this man has done nothing wrong."

Jesus, I want the assurance of Paradise this day. Would you please forgive me my many sins? Grant me the grace to be in Paradise with you.

"WOMAN, BEHOLD YOUR SON. SON, BEHOLD YOUR MOTHER."

His mother, remember I said it was when I saw her receive His broken body that the words he spoke on the cross made sense. She is quite a woman, human, yet so special. I had heard all the stories about Jesus' conception, but sometimes it is easier to believe lies than the truth. What an awesome privilege and responsibility she accepted with His birth. At the cross, I knew that Jesus wanted John to care for His mother and I knew he wanted His mother to accept John as her son. "Mom, care for Him like you cared for me". But when I placed Jesus' broken body in her arms and she looked at me, I knew, Jesus wanted her to care for me too. Do you get it? He gave me His mother too.

Mary, sometimes I feel so broken physically, mentally, and emotionally. Would you please receive my brokenness today?

"MY GOD, MY GOD, WHY HAVE YOU FORSAKEN ME?"

His wasn't an easy death. When he cried out those words, I knew they were the Holy Words of the Psalmist. But I have to tell you, I only thought of them as the words of a frightened, suffering man calling to His god. He was crying out for help in His suffering. Crucifixion is a horrible death. Breath is caught in the lungs. The agony is terrible. Anyone would call out to be saved. Why wouldn't Jesus? But I was only looking with my physical eyes at the scene before me. Since all this has happened it is as if my spiritual eyes have opened and I see differently. That Psalm speaks of this man. Jesus is this Suffering Servant. What begins as a cry of agony ends in triumphant joy. I remember the last sentence of the Psalm. It says, "Let the coming generation be told of the Lord that they may proclaim to a people yet to be born the justice he has shown."

Jesus, please encourage me by what you suffered, and allow me to offer my suffering just as you did. Grant me the courage to proclaim your justice.

"I THIRST."

How pitiful to hear Jesus say, "I thirst!" I once heard the story about Jesus and the Samaritan Woman. Can you imagine he'd talk to a Samaritan woman and ask her for water? Jesus had a way of doing the most unexpected things. He tried so often to help me see the narrow perspective I had about the ways of God. I would never have given her a drink, much less asked her for a drink. Why, I wouldn't have even spoken to her! Once more Jesus proclaims His thirst. He is trying to tell me more. I can quench His thirst by bringing the Good News to the world around me just like the Samaritan woman did. It is imperative that I know that no one is excluded from His living water.

Lord, I'm thirsting for your living waters and I know you are faithful to allow me to drink fully. Please grant me the grace to be your vessel to satisfy your thirst for souls. Help me not to keep the treasure of your love a secret from a thirsting world.

"IT IS FINISHED."

It is the Passover anniversary that all good Jews observe. We know what it means to slaughter the Passover Lamb. Sacrifice is a need of the human heart. Life as it is has to be surrendered in order to be transformed. I remember John the Baptist's words when he called Jesus the Lamb of God. Jesus is that Lamb. He is spotless. He has no broken bones, which is the sign of the perfect obedient lamb. The hour of His crucifixion is at the same time when the high priest begins to slaughter the Passover lambs. When the high priest has finished that last lamb he cries out, "It is finished!" Jesus knew he was God's lamb. He was the lamb that would take away the sin of the world. No other lamb could do this. He could cry out for the whole world to hear, "It is finished."

Jesus, I believe. It is finished. Nothing can separate us from your love, your forgiveness, and your mercy. You paid the price. Such Good news has to be shared. How dare I keep it a secret.

"FATHER, INTO YOUR HANDS I COMMEND MY SPIRIT."

When day ends and one's work is finished there is a peace that settles into our being. Our task has been completed. All that was required is finished. There isn't one thing left to do. There is no loose string left dangling. What a joy when that time arrives!

I watched Jesus when he said this last word. He was at peace, but full of energy, and able to just let go into His God. It was so inappropriate to what he had been experiencing.

I offered my tomb for His burial. That seemed the least I could do for some one who had become so special in my life. Now I know that the body that lay lifeless in the tomb is our body. The body that rose again on the third day is our body. The body that ascended above all the heights of heaven to the right hand of the Father's glory is our body. If we are not ashamed to acknowledge the price he paid for our salvation, we too will rise to share His glory. No longer is my life in Jesus Christ a secret. I want the whole world to know, Jesus Christ is my Lord and Savior.

The Last Seven Words

as heard by

The People of Sacred Heart Parish

Standing at the Foot of

The Cross of Jesus

God loved the world so much that He gave His only Son so that anyone who believes in Him shall not perish but have eternal life. God did not send His Son into the world to condemn it, but to save it. *John 3:16*
We have all heard that quote from scripture many times. But do we believe it? Today I ask you not to close your eyes as I lead you through the Seven Last Words of Jesus, but rather to look at our crucifix hanging in our sanctuary. It is a copy of the 16th century crucifix hanging in St. Peter's parish in Limpias, Spain. The corpus is 6 feet tall and if you notice the index and middle fingers, they are extended as if giving a blessing to us. What is unusual about this cross is that the Body of Jesus has not been pierced. It is as though Jesus is still alive in the midst of His crucifixion.

It was not until 1919 that, this crucifix in an almost forgotten church began to draw people's attention. Often, people reported that His eyes moved and seemingly looked right at a person. Others report that His body moved. Many miracles have occurred with this cross just by people praying before it. Today I ask the people of Sacred Heart Parish to look anew at the treasure they have in their sanctuary. Jesus hung on this cross for you and for all peoples. I invite you to stop, look and listen. Stop and be still, look at the cross before you and listen with your heart and hear the Seven Last Words of Jesus as He speaks to you anew.

"FATHER, FORGIVE THEM. THEY KNOW NOT WHAT THEY DO."

You do not know my mercy. You do not believe in my mercy. You do not believe that my suffering was for you. You do not believe that my death on this cross is sufficient. You merely nibble at these truths. How I long for you to know this truth, you are forgiven. So often you are blinded and do not even realize when you sin. The darkness of sin overwhelms you and you deny the truth of forgiveness. Satan comes with His accusing lies and you believe him and doubt my forgiveness. If only you would be open to my mercy; repent and believe your Father's desire to forgive. Do not close your eyes to the truth. Open your eyes; see me dying for you, believe the "good news" of this cross I hang on.

Jesus, I want to believe. I see you on this cross suffering for me, but no one has ever loved me that much. It is almost overwhelming to believe that you would lay down your life for me. Jesus, help my unbelief. Help me to believe that I am forgiven by your death upon this cross.

"THIS DAY YOU WILL BE WITH ME IN PARADISE."

Can you see yourself being crucified for your sins? Which of the thieves are you? Do you believe that I am sinless? The truth is you are a sinner and I AM sinless. Only I could die for your sins. Often times you deny your sinfulness, especially to save face from your friends, society and yourself. But I tell you, each of you is a sinner. Only I AM sinless. Only I could die for your sins. And I chose to say "yes" to the Father's plan and be the Suffering Servant for all of you. Not only are your sins forgiven on this cross, but I shall rise again and defeat death. Then you can spend eternity with me in Paradise. Heaven awaits all who believe and accept my forgiveness.

Jesus I want to be the repentant thief, the one who recognizes His sinfulness. I want to acknowledge your sinlessness. You didn't deserve to die. I know you are the Suffering Servant the scriptures speak of. Help me to choose Eternal Life in you. Help me to choose the Paradise you offer me.

"WOMAN BEHOLD YOUR SON, SON BEHOLD YOUR MOTHER."

I give you my Mother, my sinless Mother. She is the one who said "Fiat" to the angel, Gabriel. Her desire was to always do the Father's Will. The Holy Spirit overshadowed her and forever more was with her. My Mother loves with the purest love. She is able to ponder and bring out the riches of every situation. She is an excellent teacher. She knows mercy intimately and always desires the best for her children. She is trustworthy. I desire for you to know my mother, Mary. I desire for you to trust her with your lives. Allow my mother to lead you. She always brings you closer to me and the love we have for you.

Mary, the desire of my heart is to give all to you in total surrender. Mary, you accepted me as your child, I want to accept you as my mother. Your hands are open to me. Please allow me to take your hands and receive your embrace. Once more the key is trust, complete trust that you will lead me in perfect unity with your Son. Thank you, Jesus, because in the darkest moment of your own life, on this cross, you thought of us and left us a mother, your mother, Mary. Thank you Jesus for not leaving us orphans. Mary, I say "yes" to you being my Spiritual Mother. Come Holy Spirit, living in Mary, come.

"MY GOD, MY GOD, WHY HAVE YOU FORSAKEN ME."

Sin, dark ugly sin, surrounds me. There is no light. There is no love. God, where are you? The absence of love breaks my heart. The pain of sin overwhelms me. There is no comfort, no solace, and no relief. Darkness, chaos, and loneliness are all a part of sin. MY God, my God, why have you forsaken me? God does not abide in sin.

Jesus, I know I am a sinner. I know what it feels like when I sin and go away from you. It causes me to want to repent and run to you for forgiveness. But sometimes I choose to wallow in my sin and then usually it gets worse. I grow miserable. I can't imagine what you endured when you took on all of the sin of mankind. My little mind cannot comprehend that. Your agony has to be indescribable. Jesus only your love for the Father's Will could keep you in this place. Jesus, how could I ever repay you for all that you suffered for me? For all that you did for everyone?

"I THIRST."

The darkness of sin makes me thirst. I thirst for love. There is no love in sin. Sin is completely devoid of love. I cry into the darkness, "I thirst". Who will answer my cry? Does anyone hear me? I am thirsting for love. Please, does anyone hear me? Wow, someone hears my cry of thirst. He runs to answer my cry. He offers me wine on a hyssop branch. I drink this wine, this fourth cup of the Passover. I drank the other three cups at the Passover Meal. I told my followers I would not drink of the fruit of the vine until the day when I drink it new in the reign of God. I drink it now. My sacrifice is accepted. I will take you as my people and I will be your God. I AM the Lamb of God.

Jesus, I am not a Jew. Unfortunately, I don't understand the Pascal Meal very well. I didn't understand the significance of the drinking of the Fourth Cup. I know you refused the drugged wine they offered you at the beginning of your crucifixion and I often wondered why you would accept wine later. Now I understand. You are the bridge of love between the Jews and the Gentiles, the Old and the New. You are the Lamb of God who takes away my sins and makes me new in you. Thank you.

"IT IS FINISHED."

Yes, it is finished. I came to do the Father's Will and it is finished. All that He asked of me has been done. Just as my mother said "yes" to the angel, I said "yes" to my Father and emptied myself to become one of you, my Beloved brothers and sisters. The Father in His great mercy had a plan after the fall of Adam and Eve. My Mother and I are the new Adam and Eve. We said "yes" to the Father. There is no disobedience in us. Because of our "yes" you are able to enter Paradise. The Door is open. We call you to say "yes" to the Father's mercy. Do not allow my death to be in vain. It is finished. There is nothing more that can be given.

I say "yes", Jesus. I say "yes" to the gift of the new life you offer me. I understand the gift of my Baptism that sends Satan and His cohorts away from me. I accept your death on the cross for my Salvation. I accept the gift of the Holy Spirit and Mary who enable me to live this new life and bear much fruit. Yes, it is finished. I choose freely to give my life to you anew. Father, in your mercy hear the cry of your Son as He says, "It is finished forever and ever."

"FATHER, INTO YOUR HANDS I COMMEND MY SPIRIT."

Long ago the Son of God emptied himself of all His gifts and graces and humbled himself to become Son of Man. On the cross the Son of Man empties himself. He seeks forgiveness for us from the Father trusting in His humility that the gift of offering himself for us would be enough. Then He boldly offers us the return to the innocence of Adam and Eve, an offer of Paradise for each one of us.

Then Jesus gives us the gift of His Mother. Jesus gives us the Immaculate One to teach us how to live and be in our new self. The Holy Spirit is Mary's spouse, so we are in good hands.

The darkness of our sins covers you and you call out to God in your abandonment. Love and light are absent in the darkest of darkness, incomprehensible to our finite minds.

Out of the darkness your greatest desire is voiced, "I thirst". Jesus you thirst for our love, you long for love, and yours is an insatiable thirst. Hastily, wine is offered. A small gesture of love for the thirsting Savior.

It is consummated, only mankind can satisfy His thirst for love. Jesus longs for our love, your love and mine. Only we can satisfy that thirst.

All is finished, the message has been given. Returning to the Father is all that is left. Father into your hands I commend my Spirit. Father, Daddy, Abba it is finished. I did what you asked of me. Into your hands Father, I give you my Spirit. I trust in your timing. You will give me Resurrection Life in your time. I come to do your will. And the people of Sacred Heart Parish said, "Lord Jesus, we accept your mercy."

The Last Seven Words

as heard by

Mary, Our Mother

at the Foot of the Cross

Once upon a time there was a young woman. She loved her God and spoke with Him often. One day an angel of the Lord appeared to her and said she would conceive a child. Her answer to her God was,"Let it be done unto me as you say". She risked, obeyed and waited to see how God's Word to her would happen. She only knew she was to name her Son, Emmanuel, God with us. In time, her Son was born amidst many surprises. His birth was not what she had expected. Like all children He grew in wisdom and understanding. He loved Mary's God and called Him Father. One day He would call out in anguish to this Father. Mary was there that day. Mary watched her Son carry His cross. She watched Him be nailed to that same cross. Now her Son hung in His nakedness upon that cross. Like all Mothers, Mary, never thought when she was told she would bear a Son, that her Son would be hanging on a tree. It was difficult to recognize her Son. He had been scourged, spit upon and stripped of all dignity. There was even a Crown of Thorns upon His head. Her heart ached with disbelief, grief and deep sorrow. She was standing at the foot of the cross watching her Son in His crucifixion.

Sit back, listen with your ears and heart to Mary as she stands at the foot of the cross watching her Son die at our hands. We are all sinners. We have all cried, "Crucify Him".

Her Son, Jesus, is being crucified. Crucifixion is a torture, especially to the lungs. Breath gets trapped in the lungs and cannot be expelled. But look! With effort beyond our imagining, Jesus is raising himself up on the cross, and He speaks—

"FATHER, FORGIVE THEM. THEY KNOW NOT WHAT THEY DO."

Mary speaks, "That is my Son. Only He would forgive at a moment like this. Jesus spoke to me often about forgiveness. He said that was most important in His Father's Kingdom, His Father's Will. It grieved Him deeply when people wouldn't forgive. But He knew their hearts had to be instructed on the sin they were doing. Why I remember Him speaking about a woman He met at a well. She had been with five men and she didn't realize how offensive that was to the Father. It broke His heart to see her living like that. After speaking with her for awhile, she could see the truth. She repented of her ways and sought forgiveness. She stands at the foot of the cross with me now. She is my friend, Mary of Magdala. She knows about forgiveness. My heart reaches out to all and I pray that they could repent and find the forgiveness that is being offered to them."

Mary, we know it is easy for us to close our hearts and not see our sin. We don't like to acknowledge that we are sinners. Please pray for us to have a change of heart. Pray with us to be enlightened by the Holy Spirit to acknowledge our sinfulness. Please pray that we might have the grace of Mary Magdalene and repent and receive forgiveness.

"THIS DAY YOU WILL BE WITH ME IN PARADISE."

Mary speaks, "My Son, Jesus, emptied himself and became man in my womb. He lived in Paradise with His Father and came to earth for us. He told me He would die for us. I never thought it would be like this. Now I understand. That man hanging next to Him heard His word of forgiveness. His heart was converted and now His action is to seek that forgiveness. My Son's death will not be in vain. His words of forgiveness will echo out to all who will listen. But that other man next to Him on His cross has hardened His heart. He doesn't want to accept my Son's words of forgiveness. My Son always offers freedom. You have a will to say "yes" or "no". Today let your will choose "yes". My Son sets before you life or death. The choice is yours."

Mary, you make it sound easy, choose life or death. But we know that our will is strong. You knew how to say yes when the angel came to you. We don't trust like you do. We are cowards. We seem to prefer our will rather than trust. Pray for us, so we can say yes to your Son's offer.

"WOMAN, BEHOLD YOUR SON. SON, BEHOLD YOUR MOTHER."

Mary speaks, "What is my Son saying? He is asking me to be mother to the Beloved Disciple. Now it is I who will have to trust. My Son asks much of me. He is asking me to be mother to many children. He is asking me to extend my mothering. This is a deeper "yes" that He is asking. I am mother to all of you who have said "yes" to my Son. I am your mother. I can feel it in my bones as I did when the angel told me I would be a mother to Jesus. My womb which is barren except for my Son Jesus now will bring forth more children. I want to be mother to you. I want to teach you, lead you in truth, prepare you but mostly I want to love you into the image of my first born. Accept me as your mother. Say "yes" to my Son's offer. Consecrate yourself to me."

Mary, we never thought we needed a mother. We have known your Son, but now He leads us to you. He wants you to be known. He wants us to know the privilege of having you for a mother. Jesus isn't fearful of losing our love if we come to know you, Mary. But we are fearful. We don't want you to be a false god in our life. We love your Son. Help us to choose you for our mother. Help us to face our fears of intimacy of knowing you as our mother. Mary, help us to choose you for our mother. You are the mother of Jesus, help us to become more like Him.

"MY GOD, MY GOD, WHY HAVE YOU FORSAKEN ME?"

Mary speaks, "Time passes. Breathing has become more difficult for my Son. He is in agony. He is human and He feels the pain. He knows the psalm of the dying man. Your sin has become bone of His bone and flesh of His flesh. He has given all and He recognizes His abandonment. Abandonment, that is when the eye is filled with darkness and the soul is filled with loneliness. His cry fills the darkness. I want to run, but I cannot move. Where could I go to find comfort, solace? Who can comfort my Son? I can only gaze upon His broken body. I cry to our Father. See your Son. See His agony. I trust you Father to make good out of this."

Mary, how did you stand it? How did you stand at the foot of the cross? When suffering comes to us, we, too, want to run. When suffering comes to our loved ones, we don't want to stand with them. Suffering, darkness, loneliness, pain, and not being in control is too much for us. Mary, you said you would be our mother. Can we count on you to stand with us when we are called to suffering?

"I THIRST."

Mary speaks, "Have you ever been thirsty? Do you know only living water will quench that thirst. My Son promises living water. Jesus is thirsty. Physically His body is drying up. One cannot endure what He has been through without experiencing thirst. He refused the drugged wine they offered earlier. Remember He said at the Passover meal, "I tell you, from now on I will not drink of the fruit of the vine until the coming of the reign of God." Abandonment has driven him to the deepest desire for the Father's Kingdom, the Father's Will . That is His burning thirst. It always was and always will be. Look! They offer Him common wine on the end of a hyssop branch. And He takes it. His blood that He is offering, His very life, is like the blood that was offered on a hyssop branch to mark the doors of all who wanted to be saved at that first Passover. You my little children are the common wine, vinegary and bitter, that He must consume and change into himself. It is by His blood, shed on this cross that He will save you.

Mary, pray for us to thirst for the Fathers Will as Jesus did. Pray for us to thirst for His love. Pray for us to thirst for His mercy. It is so easy to fill our thirst with various addictions, so we don't feel our thirst for Jesus. Help us to thirst for the souls of our brothers and sisters to know you and the Father's Kingdom. Turn our thirsting into evangelizing for the Father's Kingdom.

"IT IS FINISHED."

Mary speaks, "My Son says, "It is finished." Do you understand? It is one of our customs to sacrifice Passover Lambs in the temple. The lambs are curious animals. They do not run or cry out when being sacrificed by the High Priest. It is the High Priest who cries out, "Kalah" or as you would say, "It is finished" when the last lamb is sacrificed. My Son is the sacrificial lamb for your sins. Do you remember when some people in the synagogue were angry with Jesus, and they led Him to the top of a hill and were going to throw Him over? But He passed through their midst and walked away. Now another angry crowd has led Him to the top of another hill and He did not resist. It was the Father's time for Him to be sacrificed. My Son, my faithful loving Son, my heart is pierced as I see His sacrifice. Please accept His love for you. I beg you, do not allow my Son to die in vain."

Mary, we see your grief. It is difficult to look at you. It breaks our hearts to see you grieve. His death is near. His work is finished. Mary, teach us about silence. Help us to cherish silence and ponder as you did. Mary, help us to persevere until that day when our life on earth is finished.

"FATHER, INTO YOUR HANDS I COMMEND MY SPIRIT."

Mary speaks, "My Son, Jesus, died with dignity. It has been said that how one lives is how one will die. My Son was fully man and fully God. He lived a life of love. He put into practice what He taught. His words were always spoken in truth, because He is Truth. No one took His life, rather, He went out to meet death. He always submitted himself to the Father's will. He taught me so much. He is my Son. He is my God. Our love is one. His was not a quiet, weak voice that gave up His last breath. Today my grief is deep. I mourn for all who have not heard my Son's message. I mourn for those who refuse to hear His message from the cross. Please, do not add to my mourning."

The moment has come. Can you see the mother? Can you see the Son? The silence is so profound. There are no more words to think or words to speak. There is only your response.

The Last Seven Words

as heard by

Mary, Wife of Clopas

My name is Mary; I am the wife of Clopas. I stood at the foot of the cross with Mary, the mother of Jesus. We watched her son being crucified. What an emotional day that was for me. Frankly, I couldn't understand why such a horrible death was inflicted on such a loving man. To know Jesus was to see and experience love, a rare person in our society.

    I stood beside Mary the entire time. I scarcely could look at Jesus, while her eyes were glued on Him. She was a brave woman, although like every mother her heart had to be breaking. As they nailed Jesus to the cross, I felt her body shudder as the nails were pounded, but she uttered not a sound. I stood beside Mary, but felt so unable to truly comfort her. How do you comfort someone at such a time? I could only stand there beside her. Forever the looks that passed between them will be etched in my memory. Such love they had for each other. As I said, I really didn't understand why this was happening. I knew that some of those in authority resented Him, but I never thought anything like this would happen to Jesus.

    I was with the other women in the morning after He died. We were going back to the tomb to anoint His body properly. Imagine our surprise when we saw the stone rolled back and His body gone. Then the two men in dazzling garments appeared. "Why do you search for the Living One among the dead?" They went on to say, "He is not here, He has been raised up. Remember what He said to you while He was still in Galilee— that the Son of Man must be delivered into the hands of sinful men, and be crucified, and on the third day rise again?" With this reminder Jesus' words came back to me. We couldn't wait to get back to Peter and the rest of the men, my husband Clopas included. But they didn't believe us. I didn't blame them. I, too, could scarcely believe it myself. My husband came to believe while we were walking on the Road to Emmaus. But that is another story.

"FATHER, FORGIVE THEM. THEY KNOW NOT WHAT THEY DO."

    Can you imagine? Jesus was asking for them to be forgiven. I remember that He told us in His prayer to forgive those that trespass against us so we could be forgiven equally as well. I never dreamt He meant under these kinds of circumstances. This was a very difficult word to understand. Mary didn't seem upset by what He said, but I sure was. I am not one to hold a grudge, but this was different. They were killing Him. I thought He was taking this forgiveness thing too far. There have to be limits to forgiveness.

    All this changed when I heard the message of the angels at His tomb; I realized that forgiveness is a key to His rising. Unforgiveness keeps us trapped in the death of our bitterness, anger and hatred. It affirms our pride, arrogance, and foolishness. How many times I refused to forgive. Often the person had no idea I held them in the prison of my own making, my prison of unforgiveness. Now I understand it is I who am in prison, the prison of unforgiveness. Jesus, help me to forgive my brothers and sisters. I need out of the prison I have placed myself in.

"THIS DAY YOU SHALL BE WITH ME IN PARADISE."

Jesus spoke those words to that man on the cross next to Him. Mary looked at the man and I saw a slight smile on her face. She seemed to understand why her son had spoken those words. She looked over at the other man and I saw sorrow in her face. One man was looking to escape the cross; the other voiced His desire to come into the Kingdom. Jesus was telling the one who appreciated His Kingdom that He had heard His request and was granting it. Jesus was always talking about His Father's Kingdom and how He wanted us to live in that Kingdom.

I discovered another key at the empty tomb. The Living belong to the Kingdom. One man knew His need for forgiveness and was forgiven. He was offered life in the Kingdom. The other poor fellow chose the here and now. He only wanted a Messiah that could bring him escape from His present situation. He could not think of forgiveness, much less ask for it. Jesus, help me to always ask for your forgiveness when I have sinned and forgotten the Kingdom.

"WOMAN, BEHOLD YOUR SON. SON, BEHOLD YOUR MOTHER."

I have come to know and love Mary, the mother of Jesus. She is an extraordinary woman. She is a good listener and so easy to talk with. I know she loves her son, Jesus. It is so evident. After much effort Jesus raised himself up on the cross, and spoke these words to Mary. Mary nearly collapsed. She was able to comprehend what He was saying to her. I did not understand. Why was He giving her to the Beloved Disciple? What did all this mean? Why did these words seem so overwhelming to Mary?

Again, the empty tomb was a key to help me understand. Mary never went to the tomb with us women that morning. She knew it was empty. She trusted words spoken to her even when she did not fully understand them. Her Son had said He would rise from the dead and she believed. She knew that now all of God's children would be her sons and daughters. What a ministry she was given. I know she is my mother. I know I can go to her anytime and she will listen to me and give me her help. I know she wants to lead me to her Son. She is the kindest, most compassionate mother we can have. She loves her children and gives only the best of care to us. I only wish everyone knew Mary, the Mother of Jesus. She was my friend, but now I know her as Mother.

"MY GOD, MY GOD, WHY HAVE YOU ABANDONED ME?"

How my heart ached when I heard these words. I leaned in closer to Mary as I could sense her anguish. Jesus was always talking about God as His Father. He got into a lot of trouble with people for calling God Father. As the chosen people, we weren't allowed to even say the name of God. To think His Father, His God, had abandoned Him was unthinkable. How He must have suffered to lose His God, His Father. The way He spoke those words, I could not help but think He was hurting more from that than the actual crucifixion. Oh God, where are you in this darkness?

Only at the tomb did I realize that He truly was dying for my sins. It was my sins that caused Him to experience that separation from His Father. I understand why Mary felt such anguish. I thought I was comforting Mary by leaning closer to her, but now I know her heart was being pierced by my sins, also. Sin is ugly and destructive and causes separation from our God.

"I THIRST."

It was dark, eerily dark, and out of the darkness He spoke, "I thirst". They offered Him some common wine. He took what they offered. What was that little portion of wine offered on a hyssop branch to Jesus? Somehow I knew He wasn't asking for their wine. He was thirsting for more than that. Again, I couldn't imagine what He was thirsting for. How can one satisfy that thirst of Jesus? What is He thirsting for?

Then I remembered our prayer of David that we prayed so often, "Have mercy on me, O God, in your goodness, in your great tenderness wipe away my faults; wash me clean of my guilt, purify me from my sin.— Purify me with hyssop until I am clean; wash me until I am whiter than snow." Jesus had prayed in the Garden that the cup He was to drink of would be taken from Him. That wasn't to be. He had drunk deeply and completely of the cup His Father had offered Him. His thirst could only be quenched by love. The love of His Father and the love of the one who offers even the smallest gesture of love.

"IT IS FINISHED."

Isn't it always exciting when we finish a race? Whatever we have been called to do, when it is finished, we are filled with joy. I dared to look at Jesus when He spoke those words. I would hope that you could imagine the look on His face. He had run the race. He had drunk of the cup His Father offered to Him. It was accomplished. It was finished. Despite His broken body, the joy upon His face was so evident.

I remember when I had our children. Labor was not easy. It was painful and demanding. Once the process began there was no turning back. But when the child cried their first cry, my heart filled with joy. It was finished. The joy outweighs the pain and suffering. New life has been born and joy reigns. Awe and silence follow. It is finished. Jesus knew that "It is finished".

"FATHER, INTO YOUR HANDS, I COMMEND MY SPIRIT."

The joy on His face remained, despite the darkness of the hour, despite His broken body, and despite all that He had suffered. It was amazing to see. It was somewhat bewildering to me. I have seen and experienced suffering in my life, but this was so different. He truly embraced His suffering. It was easy to see that physically He was coming to His end, yet I don't think any other man would have lived this long with the torture His body had endured. Imagine my surprise when once more He lifted Himself up on the cross to speak yet again. "Father, into your hands I commend my Spirit." He shouted those words with an energy that is difficult to explain. It was a shout of victory! It said to my heart, "No one has taken my life. The Father that I love and spoke of so often is trustworthy." He was now giving His life, His spirit, over to the Father." Father, I trust in you. Receive my Spirit." With those words, He bowed His head and He died.

That wasn't the end. The earth itself shook. The darkness parted. My emotions ran from pure joy to deep grief. Never had I felt so alive. I was in awe.

I never slept that night. All I could think of were the events of that day. I heard from some of the men that night that the Veil in the Temple that led into the Holy of Holies was torn from top to bottom. Oh, so much happened when Jesus gave up His Spirit and He died.

Early the next morning some of the other women and I went to the tomb. Jesus had risen! Do you hear me? He, my Jesus, has risen! He lives. Mary of Magdala thought He was a gardener until He spoke her name. Clopas and I encountered Jesus on the road to Emmaus. Jesus appeared to Peter. Jesus lives. Jesus is alive!!

Before Jesus' death only the High Priest could go into the Holy of Holies. With the death of Jesus that is no longer true. You are the temple of God and He dwells within you. Jesus is not dead. In your baptism, He came to dwell with you. Yes, Jesus died, but He has risen.

The Last Seven Words

as heard by

The Centurion

During the Roman Empire, crucifixion was a common practice. It is described as a cruel and feared punishment, which was never inflicted on a Roman citizen. Rather, it was reserved for slaves or for non-Romans who had committed serious crimes such as murder, robbery, treason or rebellion. Under Roman law, the offense charged against Jesus was that of treason and rebellion. In Roman practice, scourging came before crucifixion. Scourging left the person weak and hastened the dying process, as crucifixion usually took a few days.

I have witnessed many crucifixions. That is my job. I am a centurion, which means I am a commander in the Roman Army. I am a man under authority. I have responsibility for one hundred men. When I give orders, I have an expectation that the order will be obeyed. I was ordered to accompany this man Jesus to His crucifixion. He had been scourged, given the cross, and slowly He made His way to the hill. My men nailed Him to the cross, raised Him up and the process of crucifixion began. Air gets trapped in the lungs and slowly the criminal dies from suffocation. Sometimes after a few days, we break their legs. That way they can no longer raise themselves up and attempt to empty their lungs.

There was something peculiar about this man, Jesus. He never cursed us when the nails went in. Like a lamb being led to slaughter, He seemed at peace with all that was happening. He was in pain, but His pain didn't make Him lash out. That was strange behavior. Most people die like they live. This man was a criminal, but His behavior is so different from the many I've seen crucified.

He spoke a number of times from the cross. His words affected me like no other words have. When He spoke, He spoke with authority. His words seemed carefully chosen. In the silence of my heart, I can hear Him speaking again.

"FATHER, FORGIVE THEM. THEY KNOW NOT WHAT THEY DO!"

Those words were the first He spoke. I really can't explain fully how they affected me. First of all, I took them personally. It was as if there wasn't another person around and He was speaking about me. He was forgiving me! Why would a stranger want to forgive me? But then He wasn't exactly a stranger. I knew His name. Why, who hadn't heard His name and heard about the things He had been doing around Galilee. He knew I gave the order to nail Him to the cross, but that is my job. I was only doing what was expected of me. He should know that circumstances dictate behaviors. Like I said, I can't fully explain it, but I knew that He knew me and in spite of myself, He was forgiving me. I couldn't decide if I should hang my head in shame or shout for joy. It is an awesome feeling to feel forgiven. It is awesome to have the knowledge of forgiveness.

Jesus, today we pray for the grace to know and experience your forgiveness. Forgive us our many sins.

"THIS DAY YOU WILL BE WITH ME IN PARADISE."

Those men on either side of Him had been taunting Him, just like the rest of the crowd of chief priests, scribes and elders. They took pleasure in their insults and jeers. Finally, one of the criminals next to Jesus blasphemed Him, "Aren't you the Messiah? Then save yourself and us." But the other one rebuked Him, "Have you no fear of God, seeing you are under the same sentence? We deserve it, after all. We are only paying the price for what we've done, but this man has done nothing wrong." Then the criminal said to Jesus, "Remember me when you enter into your reign."Like I said before, His words seemed carefully chosen. He doesn't say He is the Messiah, but who else could offer Paradise. He tells the criminal it will happen this day. I know that crucifixion takes more than a day, so how could it happen this day? What is going on here?

Jesus, help us to acknowledge you as Messiah, capable of allowing us to enter into your Paradise this day.

"WOMAN, BEHOLD YOUR SON. SON, BEHOLD YOUR MOTHER."

While we were walking toward this hill, I saw this woman in the crowd. It was just after Jesus fell the first time. At first, when He fell He didn't see her. But His eyes looked up from the ground and she was standing close by. I saw the look they exchanged. I figured she was His mother. Only a mother would look like that at her son. She is a strong woman to come all the way with her son. Most women would have fled from the drama of this scene. Who could stand and watch a son die? I have watched many crucifixions, but I have never seen one like this. This man, Jesus, must not have any brothers to care for His mother. In their culture, the last testament is spoken in front of family witnesses. That little group gathered around the cross must be His family. Jesus uses His agony of breathing to make certain His mother is cared for. Isn't it strange? Somehow I felt like He was inviting me to care for her too. What foolishness I am experiencing!

Jesus, your mother is a very special Woman. Help us to take her as our mother. Help us to love and cherish her as you do.

"MY GOD, MY GOD, WHY HAVE YOU FORSAKEN ME?"

This man offered the other thief Paradise, and now He calls out to His God. How can you offer Paradise and be under authority to another? His God must be most powerful. I overheard some of the Jews talking that He blasphemed by calling God His Father. This man Jesus never cried out when we nailed Him to the cross. He is not condemning and harsh like the other thieves, yet He seems like He is suffering immensely because He feels forsaken by His God. Who is this God? Why would He call Him Father? Gods aren't intimate. They are to be feared. Jesus doesn't seem afraid, rather He seems estranged from the one He loves most dearly.

Dear Jesus so many of us are fearful of your Father. We had harsh and unforgiving Fathers and when you speak of your Father, we only can remember our own Fathers. Please give us the grace to embrace your loving Father, the one who gave you to us.

"I THIRST."

Knowing that crucifixions took many hours, sometimes days, my men had brought out "common wine" to drink during the long hours. Remember I told you, when we crucify someone, we scourge first. They lose a great deal of blood and they always cry for a drink to satisfy their thirst. When this man Jesus cried out, "I thirst"; one of my soldiers ran to get a sponge. He soaked it in wine, and putting it on a hyssop branch, gave it to Him. The wine was cheap bitter wine. You should have seen the look on Jesus' face. It was full of compassion, thankfulness and joy. It was as if He had been waiting for one of us to show Him some affection, to care for Him in His poorness and bring Him the wine. He had refused the wine and myrrh before His being nailed to the cross, but He seemed delighted to accept our wine.

Dear Jesus, your poor are all around us. Grant us the grace to run to their aid and comfort them as the soldier did for you. Help us to be attentive to your words spoken to us. Jesus, you need to be loved.

"IT IS FINISHED"

After Jesus took the wine, He said these words. I tell you, something was happening that I had never seen before. We came to this place about nine o'clock in the morning and now it was mid-afternoon. From noon onward, there was darkness over the whole land. Darkness does not belong in the light of day. It is as if the heavens know what is happening on this hill. I know the Jewish high priest cries out "Kalah", when the last lamb has been sacrificed. This man utters the same words, "Kalah", it is finished. What sort of man hangs on this cross? Who is this Jesus? Why does He speak this word?

Dear Jesus, in you there is no darkness. But on Calvary you took all of our darkness, our sinfulness, to the cross with you. You are the Son of Man and the Son of God. Have mercy on us sinners.

"FATHER, INTO YOUR HANDS I COMMEND MY SPIRIT."

As I told you, it was dark. Golgotha, the place of the crucifixion, is across the Kidron Valley from the Temple. Many Jews are buried in the Kidron Valley. Their tombs are visible. In daylight one has a clear view of the temple activities and the valley. The temple is where the Jews worship and offer sacrifice. Out of the darkness, Jesus utters a loud cry, "Father, into your hands I commend my spirit". He breathed His last breath, bowed His head and delivered over His spirit. Suddenly the curtain of the sanctuary was torn in two from top to bottom. The earth quaked, boulders split, and tombs opened. I tell you, my men and I, their Centurion, were terror-stricken at seeing the earthquake and all that happened. On seeing the manner of His death, I could only declare, "Clearly this man was the Son of God". Later when I trust the lance into His side, blood and water flowed out. I knew this Jesus was more than a man.

Dear Jesus, you are able to take us from our unbelief to belief in you as the Son of God. You changed the heart of the Centurion. Please, dear Jesus, change our hearts. Open our hearts that we might be proclaimers of the love the Father has for us in you, His Beloved Son.

The Last Seven Words *of* Jesus Christ

Thank you for coming to hear my Seven Last Words. I spoke those Words thousands of years ago, but those Words are still truth. I pray that your hearts will be open, your minds receptive and your spirits willing to listen deeply. Through the centuries these Words have touched many hearts. There is a power in these Words. Allow these Words to sink deeper into your souls.

In the midst of suffering, one speaks their truth. I chose to live among you. I emptied myself to become one like you in all things except sin. Sin has no place in my Father's Kingdom. Sin destroys. The tempter speaks lies. There is no truth in him. His words do not edify, build up, encourage or support. His words condemn, tear down, bring to despair, and leave you alone.

Do you believe that I came to speak these Words to you? I tell you truly, I AM speaking these Words to your heart this day. These Words are Words of transformation. My tongue was a bridled tongue. I did not speak empty words. I did not speak foolishly. I did not speak in anger. My Words are living Words. My Words come from my heart, a heart filled with love. My Words are for your salvation, not for your condemnation. My Words are truth, dependable, accurate, and life-giving. I beg you, listen anew. Hear me this day. Believe me this day. Be renewed this day. I love you, my children.

Words are most powerful. Words spoken in love are most delightful. One word spoken in love has more power than a thousand spoken in ignorance or hatred. Silence is necessary for hearing. It is true that I spoke seven times while hanging on the cross, seven times in the space of about three hours. There was silence between my Words. Minds are usually filled with chatter. Silencing this chatter opens one to hearing. I ask you to silence your minds. Be attentive to me, listen, listen deeply, allow yourself to be transformed.

"FATHER, FORGIVE THEM. THEY KNOW NOT WHAT THEY DO."

I look out from the cross, the pain is excruciating, I see my crucifiers. Yes, I see the Roman soldiers. I see the Sadducees and Pharisees, so filled with hatred and distrust. I see the frightened bystanders. I see Herod and all who condemn me. I see all who hate me. I see all who deny me. I see all my brothers and sisters who are sinners. And I say, "Father, forgive them for they know not what they do." Ignorance is rampant. They do not know who I am. They do not know that I am the Word made flesh. They do not know that I came to give them life. They do not know that I am Jesus, Son of the Father, child of Mary, baptized in the Holy Spirit, and their lover.

Heavenly Father, forgive them. Forgive their ignorance, their blindness, their close mindedness and their hardness of heart. Truly Father, they do not know what they do. You and I know the enemy, the tempter, the accuser, the liar, the one who steals. In their ignorance, they live in darkness. Unaware, unconcerned, unloving, they stumble and fumble through their lives. Father I know you hear my Word. It is my prayer to you. Father, forgive them for they know not what they do.

"THIS DAY YOU WILL BE WITH ME IN PARADISE."

Two voices are speaking. One is speaking lies. The other speaks truth. The truth comes from the one who understands His sinfulness. He is not blinded. He has an honesty and integrity. He knows who he is. He knows himself to be a sinner. Self-knowledge is a key to understanding your sinfulness. When excuses are made for your choices and behaviors, when you embrace your own falsehoods as truth, you are able to hide your sinfulness from yourself. Pride comes in many forms. Believing that you are without sin is prideful. In the silence, after speaking my first Word, the man on the cross next to me had time to embrace the words I spoke. He allowed my Word to convict himself of His sinfulness. He allowed my Word to overcome His pride. He humbled himself because of my Word. The other man hanging on the cross next to me insisted on His self-righteousness and pride. He would not choose to humble himself and admit to His sinfulness. He chooses not to hear my Word.

Father, when Adam fell, all my brothers and sisters were destined to be sinners. Through the centuries, you have been calling your children to repentance. Father, so many do not believe that they are sinners. They refuse to believe that sin separates them from your Kingdom. I have come to take their sin. I have come to set them free. Open their minds and hearts, Father. Humble them, Father. Help them to choose forgiveness by the Words I have spoken.

"WOMAN, BEHOLD YOUR SON. SON, BEHOLD YOUR MOTHER."

My mother was always obedient to the Word spoken to her. It was her "yes" that enabled me to take flesh. She trusted the word spoken to her. She allowed my Word to unfold in her life. Even now, she stands at the foot of the cross embracing my Words. She stands at the foot of the cross with my beloved disciple. He too is a listener and obedient to my Word. I give my mother to all my brothers and sisters. She will give life in the womb of her love to all. The hearts of my brothers and sisters need to accept the love of my mother for she is now their mother also. In her obedience, she gave life to me. Now she will give life to you. Like any good mother, my mother will nurture, protect, encourage, and correct you as you grow.

Father, you first gave me my mother. I grew in the darkness of her womb hearing her sweet voice and feeling her love. My coming into this world caused her pain-and-suffering. Trusting you, she embraced her life. She nurtured me. She taught me the way of her people. She made your Word come alive in me.

Under her watchful eye, I grew in wisdom. I grew in understanding. I learned to listen for your Word. I learned obedience. Father, what a gift you gave me in my mother! I desire to give my mother to those who love me. I desire to give her more sons and daughters. Father, open the hearts of my brothers and sisters that they might receive the gift of my mother.

"MY GOD, MY GOD WHY HAVE YOU FORSAKEN ME?"

The darkness envelops me, it surrounds me. There is no light in sin. It is only darkness, desolate and consuming. There is no comfort. There is no love. The imagination can barely perceive it. Separation from light, love and mercy is unbearable. My body, my soul, and my spirit recoils from the starkness. It is a void indescribable. My God, my God, where are you? It is anguish. Faith and hope are gone, lost in the darkness. The cries of the lost and forlorn can only echo in the silence of the darkness. The sins of mankind separate me from my Father. Darkness and emptiness are my food and drink.

My God, where are you? I am trapped in the darkness of sin. Is there no escape? Am I doomed forever in the darkness of the sin? Where are you? I cannot hear your sweet voice. I do not feel your arms of love. Where are you? All is lost in the starkness of sin. Where is the light? There is no light here. Where are you? All is lost. My brothers and sisters are lost in their sin. My God, my God why have you forsaken me? Where is love?

"I THIRST."

I thirst. I am so thirsty. During the scourging much of my blood was lost. When one is crucified, the blood streams from the wounds. A deep thirst results from the enormous blood loss. Physically, I am thirsty. Emotionally, I am thirsty. Spiritually, I am thirsty. In the darkness, I cry out my thirst. I thirst for love. I thirst for the Father's will. In the darkness of sin, I cannot find my Father. I thirst for the living God. Sin has separated us. I thirst for salvation for my brothers and sisters who are trapped in their darkness of sin. In my anguish, I cry out, "I thirst". In the darkness, my word is heard. On a branch of hyssop, a sponge soaked in common wine is offered to my parched lips. A small token of caring love is offered. The Father in His mercy has opened the ears of someone who will listen to my cry. He runs to give me the little he has. Little does he know the gift he gives me.

Father, you have heard my prayer. You have heard the cry of my heart. I cried out in the darkness of sin, seeking you and seeking my brothers and sisters lost and unable to love. You offered me common wine for my thirst. It was given out of compassion and love. It was the best that could be offered at the time. Compassion and love are able to chase away the darkness.

Compassion and love bring light. Compassion and love are marks of your kingdom. Thank you, Father, for quenching my thirst and allowing love, mercy and forgiveness to flow in all of my brothers and sisters, truly their sins are forgiven. A new covenant Is established.

"IT IS FINISHED."

It is done! My work is done. I was obedient to the Father. I have given my life for the sins of my brothers and sisters. I have suffered the separation from the Father. The Son of Man and the Son of God have come together on this cross. Yes, my work is done. For this was I born, Emmanuel, God with us. There is no greater love than a man lay down His life for the other. I have willingly laid down my life. It is some 2000 years later, but I have laid down my life for you today. I call you to be my Beloved Disciples. I call you to accept the work of the cross, your salvation. Do not allow my love to be in vain. The work of the cross is finished.

Father, I have completed my work. I have done all that you have ask of me. I have been your lamb. I have willingly laid down my life for the love of my brothers and sisters. I have done what you have called me to. I can say my work is finished. Now is the time for my brothers and sisters to work. It is time for them to take up their cross and follow me. I have laid the foundation. They need to build on it. I have given them wisdom. They need to cultivate this wisdom. I have taught them to hear my voice in the darkness of the lives of their brothers and sisters. They are called to share the good news of their salvation to those lost in the darkness of sin.

"FATHER, INTO YOUR HANDS I COMMEND MY SPIRIT."

It is over. I have paid the price. I was obedient to your word Father. Sin has been defeated. The last enemy to be met is death. When Adam and Eve sinned, death entered the world. Abel was the first to die. Since Abel the common thing belonging to all humans is death. It is imperative that death be defeated. Father, you are the creator, the author of life. I trust in you. I trust in you. I offer you my life. Into your hands I commend my spirit.

Death has been defeated. The cross was not the end of the story. On the third day, I rose from the dead. I am alive. Father, I trusted in you to give new life to my broken body. My disciples touched the scars where once the wounds were. I ate with them. I spoke with them for 40 days. Now I have ascended. I am seated in heaven where I await the coming home of my brothers and sisters.

The Last Seven Words
heard by
God the Father

I felt two powerful emotions as my Son, Jesus, hung on the cross that day. They were Sorrow and Joy. It is a horrible experience to see anyone immersed in sin. My Son, Jesus, was immersed in your sin and the sin of all mankind. Of course, sorrow filled my being at such a moment of darkness. There is no light in evil. What Father wouldn't feel sorrow at such a moment? The sufferings in His body, soul and spirit were unlike any other human being has suffered. He is my Son, but He also is the Son of Man. The Immaculate Mother, Mary, bore my Son. She said "yes" and Jesus was conceived in her by the power of the Holy Spirit. It is Jesus' flesh that bore the pain the Godhead, the Divine Nature of God, could not suffer.

Look at the cross and you see nails holding my Son captive. It is not the nails that hold Him. Love drove Him to that cross. It was our love for each other and our mutual love for each of you. Such Joy resulted from His offer to be one of you so that sin and death could be defeated. Jesus emptied himself to be my Lamb—The Lamb of God willing to suffer and lay down His life for each of you.

Listen. Listen deeply to my Son, Jesus, as He speaks in the depths of His sufferings. He is the Obedient Lamb led to the slaughter for your sake. Jesus desired to restore all that was lost by Adam and Eve.

"FATHER FORGIVE THEM. THEY KNOW NOT WHAT THEY DO."

"My Son has seen your sin. It is always before His eyes. He wants to offer you forgiveness. He calls to me, His Father, to forgive you. He tells me that you don't know what you are doing. Ignorance of love causes your sin. You do not know how to love. You pretend to love, but so often that love is only your selfishness. Choosing your will blinds you to our Will. Your desire is to appear "good", but you lack truth about yourself and who I AM. You do not see the specks and beams in your eyes. You do not hear our words of forgiveness and mercy. The Cross is the place of mercy and forgiveness. Open your eyes. See my Son shedding His blood for you. Open your ears. Hear our desire to forgive you for your ignorance and your selfish will. My Son, Jesus, and I, your Father, are offering forgiveness to you. Will you receive it?"

"THIS DAY YOU WILL BE WITH ME IN PARADISE."

"Two men hang on either side of my son, Jesus. They are criminals, charged for their sins against society. Their personal sin is not exposed. One is hard hearted. No light shines in His soul. He has given himself over to darkness and does not want to make a different choice. The other thief has a limited light in his soul. He hears those first words spoken and the light increases in him. He realizes he needs a Savior. He realizes he needs to be forgiven. His sin is before him. His sin against society and his personal sin are exposed. He knows he is not "good". He knows his love is minimal. He sees the righteousness of Jesus and he asks for forgiveness. My Son requires nothing more from him. The thief acknowledges his sin and asks for forgiveness. Jesus assures him of Paradise. My Son, Jesus, is willing to take your sin and give you Paradise in return. That is the price He paid for you too. Stir up the light that is within you. Will you ask for forgiveness and accept the Paradise that's offered?"

"WOMAN BEHOLD YOUR SON. SON, BEHOLD YOUR MOTHER."

"Do you know my daughter, Mary? She is worth knowing. Never was there a woman as holy as she. She was conceived Immaculate. Her "yes" to the message given to her by an angel allowed her to conceive my son, Jesus, in her womb. She nurtured, instructed, and loved Him unconditionally. She is Mother par excellent. My Son's heart and hers are in an unbreakable union. They share the same "yes" to my Will. They hold nothing back in their love. Because of her "yes" and her love, Jesus wants everyone to have His mother. He gives Mary her vocation. She is to be Mother to all my children. In return, all children are to know she is their mother. Do you know Mary as your mother? She wants to nurture, instruct and love you unconditionally. The disciples knew Mary as Jesus' mother. They knew her well. But on the cross Jesus desired to share His mother. Jesus, my son, bequeathed His greatest "good" to His brothers and sisters. That includes you. Do not shun this gift. Please, accept her as your Mother. Become her child. She will nurture, instruct and love you unconditionally.

"MY GOD, MY GOD, WHY HAVE YOU FORSAKEN ME?"

"My Son is the Word made flesh. He heard the Word proclaimed in the synagogues. His Mother and delightful Joseph taught Him the scriptures. The Word was bone of His bone and flesh of His flesh. At this time, after communicating with me on the cross, offering our forgiveness to the repentant thief and leaving His Mother as gift to all of His brothers and sisters, Jesus utters the scripture known to those of faith. Jesus quotes the psalm that speaks of His death. What was previously only words have become His reality. His bones are racked, His throat is dry, and His hands and feet are pierced. They have cast lots for His clothing, but that is not the end of the story. For the psalm goes on to say; "For he has not spurned nor distained, the wretched man in His misery, nor did he turn His face away from me, but when he cried out to His Father, I heard Him." My Son is not despondent. It is His cry of trust and joy in me, His Father. I heard my Son's pain and suffering. Do you know that when you cry out in your pain, your suffering, I hear your every word? Trust us. We are with you."

"I THIRST."

"Yes, Jesus was thirsty, physically parched, but this was not what this word was about. At the Passover Feast four cups of wine are consumed. Jesus is celebrating this Passover Feast with you. He is my Lamb for this Passover. At the Last Supper He drank the first cup which was a remembrance of your being brought out of slavery, taken out of your sin. The second cup was a remembrance of your deliverance, your being saved from your enemies. He drank the third cup of the Passover in the Garden of Gethsemane. It was His blood that was going to be shed for your redemption. Only He was worthy to drink this cup. Only the Blood of Jesus, which you are now privileged to receive at each Eucharist, redeems you. Now on the cross, Jesus cries out, "I thirst". He receives the wine on a hyssop branch, reminiscent of the First Passover. He drinks the wine offered to Him. His disciples heard Him say at the Last Supper, "I tell you. I will not drink this fruit of the vine from now until the day when I drink it new with you in my Father's reign." Jesus knows that all He has suffered, endured and offered has been accepted by me. His thirst for MY Kingdom has been satisfied. Do you thirst for my Kingdom here on earth as it is in Heaven?"

IT IS FINISHED."

"It is finished. Just as I on the seventh day finished with the work I had been doing in Creation, so too my Son is finished with the work He was called to do. In six days, I created you and all that is in my Creation. My Son emptied himself, was born of Mary, and died on a cross for your redemption. His work is finished. When the job is done, there is nothing further to do. It is finished. Jesus trusted that His work would be honored by all of mankind just as I trusted that my work was complete. Do you see my son, my daughter, we now rest? Our work is done. We call you anew. Believe the Good News!

"FATHER, INTO YOUR HANDS I COMMEND MY SPIRIT."

"It was mid-afternoon. There was an eclipse of the sun. The curtain in the sanctuary in the temple was torn. My son, Jesus, uttered a loud cry, "Father into your hands I commend my spirit." What joy filled my heart! The way was open. No longer was it just once a year the high priest could enter the sanctuary of the temple. Now all can enter. There is no longer any darkness at midday, but only light and life. My Son, my Beloved Son, knowing His work was completed embraced death, death on a cross. No longer did mankind have to fear death. The enemy was defeated. Jesus could comfortably give himself, His Spirit, over to me. He trusted me. He rejoiced with me. The angels and all of

Heaven sang His praises. We all rejoice on this glorious day when Jesus did His work, gave His all, and trusted for your future. Please celebrate with us!"

PROPHETIC WORDS OF THE FATHER

"My children, my sons and daughters, I have stood with you this day as you have heard my Son's words. Those are words to ponder. Those are words to accept. Those are words meant to go deeper and deeper into your souls as you recall them. The cross is no stranger to your lives. Some crosses are little and some very large. Do not question your crosses. Embrace them as my Son Jesus did. I assure you, I will be with you on your cross just as I was with my Son that day so many years ago. Be not afraid. Nothing, I say again NOTHING, can separate you from the love of Jesus and I, your Father."

FATHER IS IT TIME?

Jesus kept hearing a word.
He had learned from His Mother how to ponder.
And He pondered, "Father, is it time?"
He healed the sick, "Father, is it time?"
He raised the dead, "Father, is it time?"
He washed His disciples' feet, "Father, is it time?"
He went to the garden, "Father, is it time?"
The blood poured forth from His pores."Father, are you sure it is the time?"
He looked at His Mother. She'd be left all alone.
His disciples, where had they gone?
"There is so much more to do.
Father, are you sure it's the time?
A kingdom needs to be established.
My job doesn't seem done.
My Father, my God, you've forsaken me.
It can't be the time. It must be wrong.
Where did you go? What about your word?
How do I know this is the right time?
"Into your hands I commend my Spirit."
They laid Him in the tomb. There was no more time.
But the Spirit in His timelessness, continued to hover
Over the darkness and chaos and lo-
EASTER came! It had been the right time.

Made in the USA
Middletown, DE
13 April 2019